# MOTOR RACING:
## The Grand Prix Greats

# Motor Racing
## The Grand Prix Greats

*Edited by*
### BARRIE GILL

**DRAKE PUBLISHERS INC**
NEW YORK

ISBN 87749–229–8


Published in 1972 by
DRAKE PUBLISHERS INC
381 Park Avenue South
New York, N.Y. 10016

Printed in Great Britain

*To*
NICK AND PAUL

# CONTENTS

# ILLUSTRATIONS

Both Publisher and Editor wish to thank the follow-
ing for permission to use the photographs as here
indicated : No. 1, 2, 3, 4, 5, 7, 8, 10, 11, 12, 14, 15,
16, 17, 18, 19, 20, 21, 22, 23, 24, Ken Shipton, Ford
Film Library; Nos. 6, 13, Maurice Rowe, *The Motor*;
No. 9, Mike Wilkins, Ford Film Library; No. 11,
Charles Sims, *The Motor*; Nos. 25, 26, ELF Film
Library.

# BRIEFING

It is more than likely that the first motor race was run when the owner of the world's first car came across the owner of the world's second car – travelling in the same direction, along the same stretch of road.

The result has somehow been missed in the copious record books that seem to have chronicled every other aspect of motoring activity since Daimler was accused of making 'a repugnant, diabolical device dangerous to the life and well-being of the citizens' back in 1885.

What is certain is that the winner would have felt a brand-new kind of inward glee and the loser a desperate feeling of frustration. They are two piston-bred reactions which have continued to plague mankind ever since !

They are also the instincts which have inspired men to test both their courage and their fellow-man's creativity in more formalised contests than can be accurately epistled as far back as the French Grand Prix of 1905.

This book is dedicated to every man – (or woman) – who ever donned a pair of goggles; leather cap; silk scarf; crash helmet or fireproof underwear – depending on the era – and went racing in earnest in a properly organised event in the proper place.

Their efforts and their enthusiasm have made motor racing a continuing and ever-growing phenomenon of the twentieth century : a sporting laboratory which has accelerated development; thrilled millions; tested man's ingenuity and courage to the limit and still remains one of the cleanest and purest forms of sport.

It is, perhaps, the only true global sport. Even soccerless nations have staged four-wheeled contests. And today's leading drivers criss-cross the world to do battle from Monaco to Mexico City; in Austria and Australia.

Motor racing has had more than its share of legends; more than its fill of tragedy. And has certainly produced more than its fair share of heroes.

This book tells the story of just a few of its greatest exponents.

B.G.

# CORRESPONDENTS' CHOICE

*Who was the greatest? It's still the favourite debating point amongst motor sport aficionados right round the globe. Here some of Britain's leading motor writers stick their necks out to add further fuel to the flames of argument.*

| | BASIL CARDEW & DAVID BENSON<br>*Daily Express* | COLIN DRYDEN<br>*Daily Telegraph* | ERIC DYMOCK<br>*The Guardian* | MIKE KEMP<br>*Daily Mail* |
|---|---|---|---|---|
| 1 | Fangio | Clark | Fangio | Clark |
| 2 | Nuvolari | Fangio | Clark | Stewart |
| 3 | Clark | Moss | Moss | Fangio |
| 4 | Moss | Brabham | Stewart | Moss |
| 5 | Brabham | Stewart | Rindt | Hill |
| 6 | Hill | Hawthorn | Ickx | Hawthorn |
| 7 | Stewart | Rindt | Ascari | Rindt |
| 8 | Ascari | Caracciola | Hulme | Brabham |
| 9 | Hulme | Nuvolari | Brabham | Hulme |
| 10 | Foyt | Hill | Hawthorn | McLaren |

| | PATRICK MENNEM<br>*Daily Mirror* | MIKE TEE<br>*Motoring News* | PHILIP TURNER<br>*The Motor* | COURTENAY EDWARDS<br>*Sunday Telegraph* |
|---|---|---|---|---|
| 1 | Clark | Clark | Clark | Clark |
| 2 | Caracciola | Moss | Nuvolari | Fangio |
| 3 | Nuvolari | Fangio | Fangio | Nuvolari |
| 4 | Fangio | Hawthorn | Moss | Moss |
| 5 | Moss | Ascari | Caracciola | Stewart |
| 6 | Stewart | Stewart | Stewart | Caracciola |
| 7 | Brabham | Andretti | Nazzaro | Hawthorn |
| 8 | Brooks | Hill | Rosemeyer | Brabham |
| 9 | Hamilton | Brabham | Ascari | Ascari |
| 10 | Rindt | Farina | Hawthorn | Rosemeyer |

# CHAPTER ONE

# Before the Flag Falls

## *by* Barrie Gill

*Television commentator, national newspaper journa-
list and author, Barrie Gill has covered more than
sixty World Championship Grand Prix since 1961.
Born in Leeds where he graduated with Honours at
the University, he made his way to Fleet Street via
the* Bury Times *and the* Manchester Daily Herald,
*becoming motoring correspondent both for that paper
and its successor, the* Sun.

*He worked on columns with Graham Hill for three
years and is author of a motor racing anthology* The
Men. *He covered motor racing for* itv's *'World of
Sport' and became member of* bbc *2's 'Wheelbase'
team before tackling motor sport from the other side
of the fence in Ford's Competition Department in
1967. He was appointed Marketing Manager for
Ford of Britain in 1969.*

*He rejoined 'Wheelbase' as presenter in 1971; com-
mentates on motor sport for 'Grandstand' and is also
Grand Prix correspondent for the* Daily Mail.

Grand Prix drivers are a race apart! They defy categorisation.
Even newspapers find difficulty in deciding where to tabulate
their exploits : on the sports pages or the news pages.

They are sportsmen, of course. They share all the extra
rations of concentration, dedication, pure stamina and uncanny
reflexes that characterise the top golfer or the world-class
tennis player.

Many of them enjoy – and often excel at – other sports.
Jackie Stewart was an Olympic-class clay-pigeon marksman;
Graham Hill a crack oarsman; Jochen Rindt a brilliant skier.
Their hobbies rarely exclude golf, shooting, water skiing or any
pastime involving complete co-ordination.

And they can usually hold their own at card-playing – the inevitable extra-mural activity of the globe-trotting sportsman. But there are four factors which set them apart from the ace footballer, cricketer or tennis player.

First and foremost they are a very rare breed. After two tragic seasons in 1970 and 1971, there can be fewer than eighteen men in the whole world who can truly claim to be Grand Prix drivers by profession. And a mere eight of these could confidently be expected to have the remotest chance of earning a genuine Grand Prix Victory in 1972. No other sport is so exclusive and so fearfully demanding.

Secondly, they are men of depth. The world expects much from its Grand Prix giants. They are, at various times expected to display the asceticism of astronauts; the quiet courage of VCs; the flair of pop stars; the after-dinner wit of a Hoffnung or Ustinov and the wild appetite for night life of an Erroll Flynn or a Dean Martin.

With the possible exception of George Best, soccer stars are usually judged by their deeds on the field alone. No one has ever criticised Bobby Charlton or Stanley Matthews for failing to reach Churchillian standards of speech-making.

Henry Cooper and Lester Piggott have not been criticised for failing to be the life and soul of night-club parties.

But Grand Prix drivers are expected to be all things to all men : strong; silent; brave; boisterous; witty; flamboyant international heroes. This is the third point of departure. They ARE international heroes. Only a Pele or a Cassius Clay can rival the Grand Prix driver's claim to international fame.

I have seen Jim Clark besieged for autographs in a tiny village store in the mountains of New Zealand. Stirling Moss is still better known than most politicians. Why are they so famous? Why does the world show such a vicarious appetite for every facet of their characters? Regrettably the tragic uncertainty that surrounds their calling is the magnet that polarises the public's gaze in their direction.

The inescapable difference between Grand Prix drivers and their contemporaries in other sporting arenas is that no other sportsman faces such a penalty for a mistake or an accident.

It is impossible not to dwell on this at the end of a season when we have lost Pedro Rodriguez and Jo Siffert – a season with no reigning Champion to claim the tribute of No. 1 on his car because Jochen Rindt was the sport's first posthumous Champion. Of the nine drivers featured in this book, four were killed at the wheel. Stirling Moss was forced from the fray by a crash that almost took his life. Only Jack Brabham and Juan Manuel Fangio have retired gracefully and unscarred from the scene – the cheerful credit side of a sporting balance sheet with a disastrously long debit column. But longevity is not the only rule of thumb by which Grand Prix drivers measure their lives.

No one can deny the rich experiences that crowd in on the successful Championship challenger. Fame, wealth, glamour, excitement, companionship and the sheer exultation of competition at its purest are the prizes. Graham Hill – in a rare, reflective mood – once told me that the 'very uncertainty sharpens the appetite. The danger makes the value of life all the more appreciable.'

Bruce McLaren – one of the soundest, safest and most likeable drivers the world has ever known – wrote this epitaph for a lost colleague, Timmy Mayer :

'The news that he had died instantly was a terrible shock to all of us, but who is to say that he had not seen more, done more and learned more in his twenty-six years than many people do in a lifetime? To do something well is so worthwhile that to die trying to do it better cannot be foolhardy. It would be a waste of life to do nothing with one's ability, for I feel that life is measured in achievements, not in years alone.'

These were sentiments that somehow made it easier for his friends to bear his loss when the energetic Bruce was wastefully killed in an inexplicable testing accident on an empty Goodwood track.

But these are not the memories that the automotive affecionado should dwell on. Motor racing has its cheerful glory in abundance – last lap triumphs and epic drives to match the soccer fan's tales of the 1966 World Cup Final; the cricket-lovers fond remembrance of Hutton with bat or Laker with ball. And there is no story of raw courage and perseverance in the boxing ring that cannot at least be matched by racing folklore.

And there are names that are sheer magic: Segrave; Nuvolari; the Ascaris; Campari; Fangio; Moss; Collins; Hawthorn; Von Trips; Farina; Caracciola; Clark; Hill; Surtees; Jenatzy and Nazzaro.

As in every sport, there is always one argument – or, at best – debate – which will inevitably ensue when two or more true enthusiasts begin to swap memories, opinions and predjudices.

I ask you: 'Would Matthews have outshone George Best?' 'Would Pele have found a way past Frank Swift?' 'How would Cassius have fared against Joe Louis?' and 'Is Sobers really in the Bradman/Hutton league?'

I defy anyone to give a categoric, irrefutable reply to any of these questions. And if we cannot affably and accurately equate performances with bat and ball on virtually unchanged grass – how can a hapless author be expected to rate drivers whose mounts have been transformed in terms of sheer power, aero-dynamics and adhesion?

Can one really compare that impertinent achievement of Clark at Indianapolis with the 'Red Devil' Jenatzy's dusty exploits in city-to-city races?

Can one even compare Fangio with Jackie Stewart – for the aerofoiled, wide-tyred, rear engined, monocoque car must surely differ dramatically from the powersliding 250F Maseratis for example, which must have been harder to drive and yet more forgiving. Greatness surely must always be measured in context.

It is fun, of course, to *try* and enumerate ancient and modern. It isn't even futile if it spurs the enthusiast to recall and savour; discuss and deliberate.

I am grateful to the eminent scribes who have taken the trouble to compile the league table at the beginning of this book. Their preferences probably tell us as much about them-selves as the drivers they catalogue. Certainly they underline the generation gap! But if they stimulate you, the reader, into having as many amiable debates as we have had at the 'Steering Wheel Club' on the very same topic – then the patient writers have more than served their purpose.

But, believe me, it is a 'Fun-only exercise'. The choice of drivers to be featured in full in this volume is purely subjective. They are drivers whom I have admired – some from afar. And some – gratefully from close acquaintance.

My fellow scribes are friends too – men who have shared the fun, the uncertainty and the sorrow of Grand Prix reporting in strange places over many happy years. I hope our joint efforts help to convince you 'the reader' that these men deserve the accolade of 'Great Grand Prix Driver'.

Now let the flag fall and the arguments accelerate away.

# CHAPTER TWO

# Graham Hill

## *by* Barrie Gill

Graham Hill sat alone. Facing the world and baring his soul. Three of his closest rivals and friends – Jochen Rindt, Bruce McLaren and Piers Courage had lost their lives in a few brief, bitter weeks. And twelve million television viewers and an audience comprising every top sportsman and sportswoman in Britain wanted to know WHY and HOW men like Hill could continue to flaunt the same fatal odds?

There was a considered pause – and then : 'I am often asked why we go motor racing. Why we expose ourselves to these dangers. It is something that is very difficult to explain. I think there is a very basic instinct in man that we HAVE to find danger somewhere. To know where it is and just experience it occasionally. I think we find it very stimulating to do this – and in this way we have become more aware of life itself. And we get much more benefit from life by doing so !'

It was a unique, electronic confessional. Unique because no driver had ever declared so clearly the philosophic panacea that enables men like Hill to put themselves at risk every time they go to work – whether in practice, on a test day or in full-blooded competitive earnestness.

And it was unique because I doubt if any of the sportsmen in that distinguished gathering – the footballers; jockeys, cricketers; athletes and boxers amassed for the BBC's 'Sportsman of the Year' Awards – could have embarked on a soliloquy with such articulate ease and such vigorous sincerity.

But it was a job that had to be done. And Hill tackled it with the same brutal determination that has given him two World Championships and carved victories from the splinters of defeat. The same determination that carried him from a hospital bed in October 1969 to garlands of Formula One victory only 18 months later at Silverstone.

At 42, the moustached Hill – the man with the sauciest and most expressive wink in camera range – is a living legend. He is a hero with housewives. A citation of courage. The most wanted after-dinner speaker in sporting life. And a damned fine driver. His career has all the ingredients of fiction at its most rumbustious and improbable. Son of a stockbroker who has never driven a car, Graham Hill didn't drive a car either until he was nearly 24 – 'And didn't particularly want to.' So much for boy wonders and aces who are born with a silver gearstick in their mouths!

A Londoner (who stepped out of his car after winning the most important race of his comeback career at Silverstone in May 1971 and asked: 'Have Arsenal won the Cup?'), he scarcely knew that motor racing existed as a youngster. Instead he concentrated on activities that conserved his energy. In fact, he achieved most success in two sports in which he can compete sitting down! 'I must confess that when I played football or cricket at school, I always seemed to end up in goal or as wicketkeeper. I could never run very fast – I was not able to put one leg in front of the other very quickly! So I always ended up with these two jobs which I thought needed a little bit of anticipation. I think this is just a coincidence.'

His main sport was rowing – 'sitting down facing the wrong way' – a sport at which he excelled. He was the stroke that led the London Rowing Club to victory in the Grand Challenge Cup at Henley in 1953. He still wears their blue and white colours on his famous striped helmet.

It was during the lull after this successful aquatic season that Hill took the first storybook step into motor racing. He had started to drive in January of that year in characteristically unorthodox fashion. He paid £110 ($264) for a 1934 Morris 8 Tourer – assured the owner he could drive – and weaved his way home across London.

He had had no instruction; continued to experiment by instinct and passed his test two weeks later. He has never had any respect for the driving test since!

Now a fully-licensed driver, he was shown an advertisement in a magazine offering motor racing 'lessons' for five shillings (60c) a lap. Says Graham: 'I decided to have a whole pound's worth. It was a strange vehicle. It looked like a small torpedo with a wheel at each corner. I only recognised the steering wheel and the pedals. But I enjoyed every minute of it. It was the most important pound I have ever spent. Those four laps gave me sensation I have never known before. I knew there and then that I must drive a racing car in a real race. The die was cast.'

There was no easy way into racing for Hill. But his incredible self-confidence saw him through. First, he had the nerve to offer himself as an unpaid instructor – with the rich experience of those four laps. 'Remember I had had four laps. The people I was "teaching" hadn't. So I told them which was the gearstick and which was the brake. And not to put their goggles on upside down. They seemed quite happy.'

It was a beginning. Hill was near racing cars. His foot was in the door. And no one was going to close it on Hill. He threw up his job in the Development Department of Smith's – the instrument people. He wasn't receiving any money for his ambitious tinkering. He hadn't even enough money for the bus fares to get him to his new-found labour of love. And his ancient Morris had been wiped out by a van whose driver admitted that he had been 'thinking of something else at the time'.

Somehow Hill had to raise the fares. He went on the dole. The Labour Exchange hadn't met anyone like him and they didn't have much success in finding work for an aggressive young man who insisted that the only suitable vacancy for him would be 'racing driver'.

Despairingly they handed over 32s. 6d. ($3.95) of Government money per week – and Hill set off to work in a barn – together with curious ducks and chickens – boldly stripping and reassembling two intriguing Formula Three cars.

'I didn't know much about them,' he confesses. 'But at least I was learning how they were made.' His inspiration for this rural activity was the promise of a drive in one of his charges and on the 27th April, 1954, the promise was fulfilled.

The eager Hill climbed into a Mark 4 Cooper/JAP – revved up to the 6,000 rpm and was as surprised as anyone else when he found himself in the lead as the flag fell and his foot steamed off the clutch. He didn't even want to be in the lead – he would have preferred to learn what racing was all about by watching the others. Still, it was a mistaken tactic that was soon rectified by the opposition. Hill finished second and fourth in the two heats. And he thoroughly enjoyed it. But there wasn't a rush of contracts from top team managers. Hill still had a long, grinding way to go. And he was twenty-five!

What a contrast to the careers of his rivals – both in his early years and today. Bruce McLaren was born amidst cars; first raced when he was fifteen – and had won a Grand Prix by the time he was twenty-two. Hill was twenty-nine before he even entered a Grand Prix!

Jim Clark crashed his first car – on his father's farm – when he was ten. Chris Amon was driving farm trucks in New Zealand when he was eleven. And Pedro Rodriguez was a motor cycle Champion at fourteen.

The new generation of 'Hill-chasers' have had equally con-trasting entries into the Grand Prix brigade. Jacky Ickx was a motor cycle Champion at eighteen, saloon car Champion at twenty and Formula Two Champion at twenty-two.

And Emerson Fittipaldi – with a modern 'classical' motor racing education – rocketing through the ranks of Formula Four, Formula Three and Formula Two racing – found himself team leader of Team Lotus at twenty-three and won the American Grand Prix for them a month after his appointment.

There couldn't be a more pointed contrast to the Hill saga with Lotus. Hill started working for the infant company for a pound-a-day; wandered off to help various assorted drivers with their cars and rejoined them as a full-time mechanic in 1955. He was paid £9 ($22.70) per week – but there was the extra-bait of an opportunity to race a Lotus Mark II sports car – provided Graham built it himself. Perhaps the yellow paintwork wasn't the only reason for its nickname – 'The Yellow Peril'. The Champion-to-be was even black-flagged at a Brands Hatch meeting for spinning the car four times on consecutive laps. Hardly an auspicious start to a career – but Hill, nevertheless, nearly won the *Autosport* Championship.

Unfortunately, Colin Chapman regarded him as too useful a mechanic to waste his time racing and Hill quit Lotus in 1957 to start swapping his services for prospective drives all over again. It took the intervention of John Cooper – who gave Hill a Formula Two drive – to prove to Chapman that Hill really had something. It is to Chapman's credit that he quickly re-signed the wandering Londoner – this time as a fully-fledged works driver. With a £1,000-a- year ($2,400) retainer from Esso.

Graham's first Grand Prix was at Monaco in May 1958. Nearly five years after those all-important four-laps-for-a-quid. No one could accuse him of being impatient! It wasn't a glorious début either. His back wheel fell off. One hundred Grands Prix later – at Monza in 1968 – Hill celebrated his centenary in the same way. His wheel fell off. Said Graham sourly : 'No one can accuse me of inconsistency.'

Hill's early Lotus days were anything but successful and in 1960 he joined BRM. Two more fruitless years followed. He had not set the world on fire and the man-in-the-street seemed to know and care for only one racing driver : Stirling Moss. 1962 was to change everything. By an ironic coincidence Hill was to win his first Formula One race – nine years after those four laps and no one would notice it! It was at Goodwood, the famous Easter Meeting.

The world doesn't remember his first victory. They were too concerned with an incident – as Hill was – that filled the BRM's mirrors : Stirling Moss's tragic exit from motor racing. It happened right behind Hill. He watched horrified as Moss drew level with him – out of control – and hurtled head-on into the banking.

Hill drove determinedly on to win. But all that mattered was Stirling Moss. The British motor racing scene – not to mention the world sporting stage – was left with a colourless void. Stirling Moss WAS motor racing as far as most people were concerned.

Who could put back the personality, the flair, the popularity and the success that Britain needed? The answer was to be given in vivid form – just a few weeks later at the Silverstone International Trophy Meeting (a meeting that seems destined to mark milestones in Hill's career). Jimmy Clark – most people's favourite to take over the Moss mantle – shot into one of his characteristic leads. As the race drew to a close, Hill was twenty-five seconds behind him. And the new Type 56 V8 BRM was in trouble. Exhaust pipes were dropping off all over the place. Then it began to rain.

Hill – with only three exhausts left out of eight – began to close the gap. With six laps to go he was seventeen seconds behind. Most drivers would have shrugged off the situation as hopeless. At the start of the last lap, Hill was still four-and-a-half seconds behind. On the sweeping Woodcote corner – yards before the finishing flag – he was still behind. Clark saw Hill in his mirrors and 'shut the gate' on his inside where the track was fairly dry. Hill chopped across to his outside – hit the wet track – broadsided past Clark and took the flag sideways, sensationally – and FIRST.

The crowd went wild. The journalists couldn't believe their eyes. It happened right under the press box.

Britain had a new hero.

I have dwelt on this race – and these frustrating early years – because it is vital to see the Hill career in perspective. Today he is a world figure. No motor racing function is complete without a few dynamic words from the best raconteur in the business.

No public poll on sporting favourites is complete without Hill – taking his place with Henry Cooper, Bobby Charlton and Tony Jacklin, as star for all tastes. No motor race is complete unless Hill flies in – jaunty, determined and personable. How has it happened? What makes Hill the epitome of courage; the essence of wit?

Ask any other driver and they will – in seconds-produce one word : determination. And add dedication, doggedness, application and even 'sheer bloody mindedness' as instant riders. The guts of Hill are that he simply won't give up. He never knows when he is beaten. And if he is beaten, he can't wait to start all over again to reverse the result.

He is a perfectionist – an irritating, aggressive, infuriating perfectionist. And it applies to everything he does : writing or water-skiing; shooting or golfing, or talking. He sets himself incredible high standards and expects everyone around him to strive for similarly elevated standards. And he loves racing. 'It's not so much the speed that's the attraction, it's the control over the machine.

'It's very difficult to describe but sometimes – when you really get a grip on the car and get right on top of it; when you can do exactly what you want to do and you're doing everything just right – it gives you a lot of satisfaction. It's a sort of mastery over the controls and the elements and the machine.

And then you've got the other fellows – the competitiveness. You've GOT to come out on top and beat them. And that adds further to the attraction. You have to try for perfection all the time. There can be hundreds of corners in a race and they change every time according to your speed, your position, the state of the track and the situation in the race. But when you really take a corner perfectly, you feel satisfied. Then, of course, you try to do it every time. You will never do it. You will never reach perfection. But you are always looking for it. Always trying to obtain it. And never actually getting there.'

This search – this driving force – is the inner engine that keeps Hill going. And it isn't blunted by the tragedy that could lie round the corner and the terrible personal losses he has suffered. Nobody meant more to Hill than his great rival and friend, Jimmy Clark. 'When he died I felt vulnerable. Everything came home to me with a terrible jolt. I just felt empty. It is a terrible time for any driver. It is very difficult to describe loss and how it affects me. One has just got to draw a blanket across it.'

Hill responded to Clark's death in grimly determined fashion. They were now team mates in the Lotus camp. Clark's death affected the motor racing world more deeply than any other of the sport's tragedies. He was the indestructible one – 'It couldn't happen to Jimmy.'

The Lotus team arrived at the next race – the Spanish Grand Prix – without Colin Chapman. He simply couldn't face it. Hill was never more determined. In a desperate duel with Denny Hulme – Hill won. It was his first Grand Prix victory since October 1965.

It was a win for Jimmy. A vital victory for Lotus. He went on to win at Monaco. And in the last race of the season – the Mexican Grand Prix – he took the title for the second time. The world recognised the self-discipline behind the conquest. The new Champion received the OBE from the Queen, and from the British public the runners-up position to Olympic Gold Medallist David Hemery in the BBC 'Sportsview' poll.

Said Graham : 'You have to learn to cope with fear. You have got to control it. I get afraid and everybody gets afraid. I think every normal person gets afraid. If you don't then you won't last very long. How do I control it? I have no set way. I can't say that I turn a switch and turn off fear. You have got to get on top of it. You have got to have confidence – confidence in yourself, your car, in the mechanics and the designer. This helps enormously. But you have got to have inner confidence too.'

Lord knows how much confidence a man needed to overtake Jimmy Clark in that race at Silverstone in May, 1962. A new boy in the Press Box, I watched amazed as he hit the puddles and slewed across the line ahead of the astonished Clark. I spent the next day recounting that last lap to everyone in the *Daily Herald* office. I pleaded with the Editor to sign him as a regular Saturday morning columnist. I let my enthusiasm run away with me. 'He'll be World Champion – I promise you.' The reply was caustic – 'He'd better be!'

Days later I confronted the new, literary Hill in the bedroom of the hotel where he was staying for the Belgian Grand Prix. The first Graham Hill column was to be created. Nervous of missing a single golden word – I had taken a tape recorder along. He talked non-stop for an hour. There were enough home-truths to fill three or four columns. Then we decided to do a replay. There was silence. I frantically re-wound the tape and tried it at every point. Not a sound was heard. The microphone hadn't been plugged properly!

I spent the rest of the night trying to recall everything he had said so that I could phone over the column first thing in the morning. Graham altered every other word. It was a hell of a way to start a partnership!

Ten years later – Graham Hill wrote his own book. Presumably using a tape recorder that worked. His inscription in the copy he sent me reads 'As a permanent reminder of the day the tape broke – and our friendship began.'

Armed with a notebook and at least eleven pens, I trailed Hill for a year as he fought, scratched and clawed for the title. At Zandvoort he gave the BRM only the second Championship victory in the British firm's troubled life. He took it very calmly indeed. 'I owed them this victory. I should have won the British Grand Prix for BRM two years ago. Perhaps this will help to straighten the account.'

BRM needed a victory. The team had been warned that if

there wasn't some sniff of success there wouldn't be a BRM team in 1963.

Tony Rudd, the mechanics and the backroom boys at Bourne spared nothing that year. And the *Herald* column was inevitably dictated at 2 a.m. in the morning as Hill sat on the wheel of the car after spending the night working with the mechanics. They had to pull out all the stops – for Colin Chapman had provided Jimmy Clark with a new monocoque Lotus 25, a revolutionary car which Clark exploited to the full.

Graham Hill had more than his share of disappointments. At Monaco, where he was later to achieve so many victories – he built up a massive 45-second lead over Bruce McLaren. But he was losing oil and with only $7\frac{1}{2}$ laps left, 13 miles in all, the engine gave up the ghost. Graham was second in the Belgian Grand Prix; ninth in the French (after a shunt); fourth in the British Grand Prix and arrived at the notorious Nurburgring with a one point lead over Jim Clark – 19 points to 18.

Before practice he dictated a graphic column on the dangers of Nurburgring circuit – with its swoops and bumps and its 170 corners. But he was nearly killed by an unnecessary, criminally careless, hazard. In practice, he rounded a hedge at nearly 140 mph down the 'Foxhole' descent to smash into a TV film camera which had fallen off its mountings on the back of a Porsche. The camera smashed the BRM's oil tank; the car spun into a ditch and careered on for a hundred yards before Hill could clamber from the wreckage.

Everybody was very shaken and there were a lot of angry words. And raceday did nothing to calm anybody's nerves. Nürburgring was at its nastiest! Torrential rain – low clouds; evil-looking mists and a delay of 45 minutes because some of the earth bankings collapsed and spilled on to the track.

Hill grabbed the lead at the start of the third lap and held it for 183 miles under incredible pressure from John Surtees and Dan Gurney. It was a classic battle through the mists. I have never seen Graham looking as drawn and drained after a race, but he had established that 'dogged' and 'relentless' reputation for all time.

Monza presented Graham with a comparatively easy victory in the Italian Grand Prix, but Jimmy Clark took the American Grand Prix by eight seconds. The duel would reach its climax in South Africa. And if Jimmy Clark won that race, the Championship would be his.

In between were ten interminable weeks of waiting. I dreaded driving to Graham's Mill Hill home to keep the column boiling. He wanted to talk about anything but the Championship. That ten weeks were the longest I have ever known – no wonder footballers don't like the gap between the semi-finals and the Final of the FA Cup!

Graham turned up trumps however. He wrote columns on headlight hazards, American driving, the L-Test, mud flaps and cats eyes. He seemed glad to talk about anything but racing. By the time we got to South Africa he had built up a defensive mental wall. We had to spend Christmas in East London. Graham and I were invited to an enthusiast's home. We were both glad we didn't have to have a hotel Christmas – but our host Bob Kershaw could never have anticipated what a fantastic guest Graham would turn out to be.

Graham has proved himself a worthy cabaret star on many occasions since that sweltering Christmas – but I will never forget that family show with the World Championship just four days away. He sang to a toy guitar. He played the tea chest bass while the grinning Richie Ginther played the drums. And he taught all the local girls to twist – then that strange new dance from England.

By the end of the evening, he was relaxed enough to turn to me quietly and say: 'You know, Jimmy's got the faster car. You mustn't be too disappointed if he wins the Championship.'

Graham was right of course. Jimmy Clark made a fantastic start and pulled out an ever-increasing lead. Then on Lap 59 – there was a puff of blue smoke. A tiny metal plug had worked loose in the engine casting. A 27 seconds lead was lost. Graham swept by as Jimmy pulled into the pits, and the Championship was his.

Graham Hill became the first Englishman to take the title in a British car – the BRM. The car that had been a joke in the racing world. The car that was now saved from extinction. Said the sporting Jimmy Clark: 'We all wanted to see BRM win something – but this is ridiculous.'

Graham was strangely subdued. 'How do you feel?' I asked him. 'I think I've got a cold,' he said.

Next morning I learned the reason for his lack of enthusiasm. During his lap of honour the crowd had pressed forward so hard that a small boy had been pushed under the back wheel of Graham's car. Graham postponed his flight to New Zealand the next day to visit him in hospital and continued to correspond with him for a long time afterwards. It was his first act as Champion.

His second titled experience was to spend New Year's Day in jail. He and Innes Ireland flew on to New Zealand via Nairobi – a fact that disturbed the authorities in Karachi no end, because they hadn't had any yellow fever certificates. They were sprayed with disinfectant; pushed into barred cells and fed eggs and brandy while soldiers guarded them with fixed bayonets until their BOAC plane arrived. 'Such is fame,' grinned Graham when he told me the story.

The Championship changed Graham – to the eternal benefit of motor sport. Despite a disastrous 1963 season in which Jimmy Clark and the Lotus dominated the Championship, Graham seemed to grow both in confidence and stature with his newly won title. Stirling Moss summed it up : 'Graham as Champion will be wonderful for the sport. He has the personality to match the position.'

Graham has never looked back. His aggressiveness softened and his wit became world famous. He won the legendary Indianapolis 500 Race at his first attempt in 1966 – and conquered America with his victory speech.

He began to monopolise one of the toughest circuits in the world – Monaco – scoring a hat-trick of victories in 1963, '64 and '65, and adding two more in 1968 and 1969.

And it was at Monaco – in 1965 – with a hat-trick in the offing, that he spelled out the Hill character for all the world to see. He was leading with a quarter of the race – twenty-five laps – safely under his belt. Then he reached the notorious chicane to find it blocked by a car limping back to the pits.

He could only stamp on the brakes at 95 mph and skid thankfully down the escape road. It was a body blow – and the angry Hill leapt from the car – then pushed it back to the circuit and set off again in grim pursuit. He had lost a massive

AN INCREDIBLE ESCAPE

One of the most serious crashes of Graham Hill's career. An aerofoil
collapsed in the Spanish Grand Prix at Barcelona in 1969 – and Ken Shipton
was on the spot to record the impact, and the escape.

### A LOBSTER AT HOME

They call the 1971 Brabham-Ford 'The Lobster-Claw' – thanks to its unique nose. At the wettest Grand Prix in years, the Dutch Grand Prix, it should have been at home but Graham Hill found it a handful.

### HELPING HAND

From 1962 until 1968, the rivalry between Graham Hill and Jim Clark was the essence of every Grand Prix – both on and off the track. But it was a duel that epitomised the sporting nature of motor racing. Here Jim Clark joins in the revelry to celebrate Graham Hill's victorious homecoming from Indianapolis in 1966. Clark finished second.

33 seconds and been relegated to fifth place. He passed his team-mate, Jackie Stewart; broke the lap record again and again and by lap 53 had caught and passed John Surtees in the second-placed Ferrari.

Ahead of him lay Bandini – with the hordes of Italians who had crammed across the border into Monaco screaming encouragement. Hill passed him, fought off a fresh challenge from Surtees, set a new race record and, of course, claimed the lap record.

There is a tiny bar in Monaco called the 'Tip-Top'. That night it was awash with beer and Graham Hill sang his rudest songs from the table-top. Two gendarmes walked purposefully forward – saw who it was – applauded him and accepted a beer before they left. Graham Hill was the uncrowned monarch of Monaco. Yet he was such a perfectionist that he told me : 'I wish Jimmy had been here – it would have been a more complete victory to have beaten him too.'

Jimmy was, of course, in Indianapolis. Next night Graham sat waiting for the result. When he heard that Jimmy had become the first Briton ever to win the race he took us all to dinner at 'Le Pirat' down the coast. To celebrate not his, but Jimmy's victory.

By 1967 Jimmy and he were team-mates for the first time. Graham left BRM to rejoin Lotus. 'I am ready for a change,' he said. 'If I stay at BRM much longer they will paint me green.'

He left BRM a name to be respected, with ten Championship victories and a World Title on the honours board at Bourne.

He and Jimmy Clark were the first drivers to use the Ford-Cosworth engine which was to keep Britain ahead of the game for many a year. Graham grabbed pole position with it on its first outing – the Dutch Grand Prix 1967 – and Jimmy won the race.

In 1968, Graham gave the engine its first Championship with a memorable last-gasp win in Mexico. It was a victory that meant even more than the Championship to him. For it evened the score.

In Mexico in 1964, the Championship was still unsettled. All that was certain was that a British driver would win it –

and the Duke of Edinburgh was present to see whether it would be John Surtees, Jim Clark or Graham Hill.

Graham had only to grab four points – a third place – to make sure of the title; even if Clark or Surtees won the race. Despite a poor start – because the elastic of his goggles broke on the grid – he quickly worked his way through to the essential third place. The title was his, until the Italian driver, Bandini, collided with him at the hairpin. One of the BRM's exhaust pipes closed up and Hill had to pull into the pits.

The mechanics were in tears with disappointment and anger. It was left to Graham Hill to walk over to Bandini at the end of the race – when Surtees was being crowned Champion – to tell him : 'Forget it – it's just one of those things that happen in motor racing.'

Four years later he put the record straight. Once again the title was wide open. Stewart, Hulme or Hill would end the day as Champion.

There was no comforting third place to aim for – Graham had to win outright to make sure. He had a furious battle with Stewart, took the lead and then with two laps to go, history nearly repeated itself, Rodriguez – a lap behind but possibly anxious to impress in front of his home crowd – hammered into the hairpin and almost hit Hill. Graham had to swerve violently to emerge unscathed – and thankfully, if not politely, waved Rodriguez past. It was an immensely satisfying victory at the end of a tragic season and at 39 Graham was Champion again.

A year later it looked as if his racing days had ended. In the American Grand Prix at Watkins Glen his right-hand rear tyre collapsed as he headed down the straight. The car shot out of control, hit a bank and ejected Hill. He had broken his right knee, dislocated his left one, torn the ligaments and damaged the nerves. He still had his sense of humour though. Always somewhat bandy since a motor cycle accident he asked the doctor : 'Can you straighten my left leg while you're at it? It will make life easier for my tailor.'

The reaction of his friends – his real friends – was very revealing. Amidst the relief that the accident had been no worse, appeared the comforting thought : 'Now he will retire.'

After all, Hill was nearly 40 – and he had had a damned good run.

But they totally misjudged the man and his mood. Once back in a British hospital, Graham made it abundantly clear that he was going to race again. His friends and admirers played along with him. After all, it would help to speed his recovery. But Graham wasn't bluffing.

A few weeks after his return, the Ford Sport Club members voted him their Ford Sport Fanfare – 'For the most popular achievement of the year,' Graham's sensational FIFTH win at Monaco. Thanks to the electronic enterprise of the BBC 'Wheelbase' team and the co-operation of Graham's doctors, the Ford Sport revellers were able to 'visit' Graham en masse via the TV camera.

As they made the presentation, Graham appeared on a huge screen – safely tucked up in bed – but as hilarious as ever. His speech was one of his best. But as he 'received' his award – a painting showing all five Graham Hill victory cars at Monaco – he declared : 'Save room for a few more. I intend to win there again !'

His next move was even more melodramatic. From his hospital bed he 'transferred himself' from the Lotus team to the Rob Walker team. It was almost unbelievable. Imagine a football manager rushing to a hospital to sign a player with two broken legs.

Soon he had more shocks. He decided to fly to South Africa to 'recuperate'. As soon as he arrived at the Kyalami Ranch – a few miles from the famous Grand Prix circuit – he borrowed a bike. And began to pedal to the track to strengthen his legs.

The inevitable happened. First, he practised the Rob Walker car. Then he declared he would race it. Brian Redman sat by in his overalls ready to take over half-way. But this was one race – with himself – that Graham intended to finish. He did. And finished well. He crossed the line sixth, to win himself a World Championship point – just four-and-a-half months after the accident that looked like 'finis'.

He stepped from the car, declared it 'the most important Championship point I have ever earned' – and clambered slowly up three flights of stairs to make a radio broadcast.

'Do your legs still give you trouble?' I asked nervously. 'Only if I walk or stand on them,' he replied with a resigned grin.

Graham Hill was back – and his comeback courage fired the imagination of both nation and media – in that order. He became a TV regular – not only on motoring programmes but on quiz shows, too. He finished his long-awaited book – and it was pure Hill in every word.

On the track he pressed on regardless – fourth in the Spanish Grand Prix, fifth in the Belgian and sixth in the British. And off it too, golf, shooting, cycling – anything to strengthen his legs.

The season ended. Jack Brabham announced his retirement. Would Hill quit too? At the January Ford Sport Ball – which Hill was able to attend without the aid of television! – he presented the Club's Fanfare Award to Brabham. It was a picture of Jack's victorious car at South Africa. Said Graham : 'I hope it's as successful this year.' Quipped Jack in reply : 'Then all you'll have to do is paint a moustache on this painting.'

The secret was out. Hill, far from retiring with Brabham was to take his place. 'I enjoy racing. I'm not a bloody invalid. I intend to go on racing as long as it gives me pleasure. Of course, if I started losing all the time – I would think again. I reckon that would take some of the joy out of it !'

He grinned – a grin that stated categorically that he would be winning again very shortly. On Easter Monday at Thruxton, he fulfilled the promise with a dramatic 0.6 second win in a fiercely contested Formula 2 Race. And the crowd went wild.

At Silverstone on May 8, 1971 – at the International Trophy Race where he had first dominated the headlines with that last gasp win nine years earlier – Hill's dream came true. He won a Formula One race again – and won it after a glorious double duel with Rodriguez. 'I don't suppose there is any victory which has given me greater satisfaction,' he said seriously. 'To win a Formula One race again after the accident, the hospital . . . it means a lot.'

It meant a lot to the crowd too. They cheered him to the echo as he toured triumphantly round the track. And Hill responded in true Hill fashion : 'I'd like to thank everybody who has made this victory possible : Jackie Stewart for crashing;

Ford, Goodyear, all at Brabham's and – of course – the girls here today!'

'Mr Personality' was back on full song. He still can't press on the brakes too hard. He still walks with obvious difficulty. But he's back in the winning seat with two ambitions: 'To win another Grand Prix – then a few more' – and – 'To live to be a hundred.'

Amen to that!

For the sport may have had better drivers; may have had faster drivers. But the sport has never had a more determined driver; a more courageous driver or a better ambassador. 'You get out of the sport what you put into it,' says Graham.

Motor sport has been presented with colour, personality and with courage by the man who won't give up – who doesn't know what it is to be beaten.

His centenary celebrations could be quite something!

# CHAPTER THREE

# Stirling Moss

## *by* Geoffrey Charles

*Born in 1925, Geoffrey Charles graduated from local papers (after serving in the RAF 1942–47) to the Press Association, then in 1952 to The Times, doing Parliamentary and political reporting, general news and features, at home and overseas. He was the Motoring correspondent 1961–70, and joined Ford of Europe in May 1970.*

Were I to achieve nothing more in my life, I could depart proudly in the knowledge that I have known personally the two greatest men in contemporary politics and motor sport: Winston Spencer Churchill and Stirling Moss.

Both will be remembered as perfectionists in their own art, supermen to whom 'life' could have but one meaning – living, at nothing less than one hundred per cent. Incredible as it might seem to some political or sporting observers, the two had more in common than many of us may appreciate. Indeed, even though generations lay between them, and their views were poles apart on many aspects of life, were they to have switched roles I believe we would still be writing of them as world-renowned figures.

Each has earned a niche in history as a controversial, tireless, extrovert character. Churchill changed (and, many of us believe, saved) the face of the world in which we now survive. Moss, still a living legend at the age of 41, unquestionably wielded the greatest influence on motor sport of any driver in the post-war era. Churchill's power lay in words, thoughts, and perception. The secret art of Moss as a driver was his uncanny faculties of reaction, skill, judgment and vision, both mental and physical, laced with an acute business sense. To each, these were inborn qualities, rarely combined in one single human being. And to each, Britain and all that it stands for, reigned supreme.

Ten years of international race reporting inevitably tempered me to the tragedies and triumphs of the world's most dangerous sport. But even now, nearly ten years later, I still shiver in recalling Goodwood circuit on Easter Monday, 1962 – the scene of Stirling Moss's last race ... the unearthly silence as news of that 120 mph crash filtered through ... the long wait ... an ashen-faced Graham Hill plodding disconsolately through the paddock ... the painful process of telling the world.

It was a blow that struck us to the heart, its enormity barely lessened as the consequences of his injuries were spelt out in the days that followed. Moss's miraculous survival and recovery can be counted as the legacies of superb surgery and the man's own determination and philosophy towards living. Moss himself admits that he never understood the mistake that almost robbed him of life. 'I make mistakes,' he says, 'but not when my life's at stake ...'

Perhaps it's irrelevant, even morbid, to dwell on that fateful milestone in Moss's life today. I do so simply to make the point that whereas to those of us involved in the sport it spelt the end of an unrivalled career for a star and hero, to Moss himself it became a stepping-stone into a new career – albeit as an international businessman, a jet-set executive, a multi-company director – the career that he would sooner or later have adopted, regardless of that inexplicable stroke of fate. For Moss never stands still.

Although in this book I should not perhaps say it, I am bored with the argument on who is, or was the greatest in motor racing. Qualification must come into any such vote. Fangio? Yes, if you count up World Championships. Clark? Yes, if you are looking at a natural talent and lightning rise to stardom. Nuvolari? Stewart? Moss ...

Yes – unquestionably Moss, if we look at him not merely as a Grand Prix ace but as an all-rounder – a point that is too often overlooked by analysts of the Grand Prix scene. It may sound almost derogatory, but Moss was not *merely* a Grand Prix driver. Remember? True, he started as many of the all-time greats have, in a very small way, on motor-cycle-engined

39

500 cc Coopers back in 1948. But in the 14 years that followed, we saw him in just about every type of motor sport – hill climbs, speed trials, Grands Prix, sports car races, saloons, international rallies, sprints, land-speed record attempts – the lot. Over that period, Moss competed in a total of 466 events. He was placed in 290. He won 194. Taking the analysis a stage further, he finished 307 races in first, second, third or fourth place, which adds up to 65.8 per cent placings. Without attempting comparisons, I would wager that no other driver has come near that record across the whole motor sport board. Moss must have been the greatest all-rounder.

Stories of Moss through the eyes of his contemporaries must have filled a million pages. But there is one man who perhaps got closer to him in action than all the rest – my old friend Denis Jenkinson, of *Motor Sport*, who rode to victory with him in a Mercedes in the 1955 Mille Miglia. Listen to Jenkinson on his 'chauffeur' : 'As a driver he was faultless, as a person he could be tiresome. No matter what the car was he instilled a fantastic feeling of confidence in me, and even though we had numerous racing accidents together, none were serious and I never lost my confidence in his ability to handle a car under any conditions ... Moss seemed to take me into a different world, doing things with a car that I could not foresee, deliberately provoking slides at times when I would imagine he would not want it to slide; forcing the car to do what he wanted it to do, rather than working at high pressure to keep abreast of what the car wanted to do ... His faculties of eyesight, judgment, anticipation and reflexes were all of an outstandingly high order and worked in rare unison. These were natural attributes that made him a super-man and in consequence very difficult to live with when not racing.'

Difficult to live with ... ? I would guess this is a classic understatement when it relates to Moss. But it could equally apply to any of these dynamo-supermen. They don't even understand the meaning of relaxation as most of us interpret it. I have never seen Moss relaxed for more than five minutes. Correction – one minute. He moves, thinks, talks, reads and lives like a cascade down a rocky mountainside – never still for a second, his mind and actions shooting off in a dozen directions almost simultaneously. While we sit, he stands. While we walk, he runs. While we ponder over a complex question, he has found his answer, run through all the supplementaries and is already ferreting out another subject.

Whatever he does, be it water-skiing, cycling, travelling by jet or dancing, Moss flings his whole mind and personality into the action. Have a coffee or a Coke with him, and while you are taking the first sip he has taken six, a skip round the table, answered three phone calls and scribbled a note to his secretary. In Moss's presence you feel either as invigorated as a Dexedrine addict, or depressingly outpaced, even lazy. Jenkinson again hits the point, when he says : 'From leaving school at a relatively early age he had lived a completely artificial life of travel, hotels, publicity, glamour and racing; after a week or ten days of this non-stop high pressure I would have to leave him and go away to regain my sense of proportion, and sit in the sun and read a book, or just sit and cogitate – something that Moss could not do and would not let his companions do.'

A conversation with Moss is like chatting to a multi-channel computerised walkie-talkie tape deck. Throw out a few comments on circuit safety, aerofoils, Annabel's, sex and speed limits, and back at you like shrapnel come his reactions, punctuated by 'boy' and 'man' – used as commas, dashes or exclamations – 'Christ !' 'Okay,' 'Yes,' 'Right !' and 'Jeesus !' It is all crisp, fast-flowing Haileybury English – amusing, fluent, thought-provoking. Yet, unbelievable as it may seem, Moss is by nature a shy introvert, for whom the whole process of learning to speak eloquently and to hold an audience – as he can do with such apparent ease – was a painful, self-taught chore.

All this electric energy transmits itself to, and invariably stimulates, those with whom Moss comes into contact.

In his racing years one could watch the whole team spring to life as he came on the scene for practice or the race. The man is infectious – in the nicest sense – yet at the same time he can be deeply serious. Always, he is meticulous in attention to detail, aiming constantly at perfection in all that he does.

To see Moss in action at the wheel was to watch a master craftsman at work. The entire process *flowed*; the man and the car were a single unit. On every corner he would clip the same spot to within an inch on every lap. While his opponents slammed, slid and wove impressive patterns through the curves, Moss melted through almost unobtrusively, but slashing seconds and minutes off their times.

Moss, as I said, like Churchill, was and is fanatically patriotic, which is why he insisted on driving only British cars on the Grand Prix circuits. This adamant patriotism undoubtedly cost him three world championships, yet who could argue convincingly that it was a wrong attitude? Enzo Ferrari, who classed him as the greatest driver in the world, was practically on the point of drawing Moss into his Grand Prix team at the time of the 1962 accident. He had undertaken to build a car that Moss wanted. 'If you drive for me,' he declared, 'I will have no team, just you and a reserve driver. With Moss I would need no team.'

Looking back, we may wonder whether the deal might have been clinched but for the Goodwood disaster. Even Moss himself isn't sure. 'I think it would be anti-climactic, winning the world championships on an Italian car after all these years,' he told Ken Purdy in his self-portrait book, *All But My Life*.

I recently spent a couple of hours with Moss in London, looking back over the years since that tragic day at Goodwood. Since then, he has developed a completely new career – as an international business tycoon (though he would probably cringe at the label). We ran through his multifarious business interests. 'Let's see now,' said Moss, 'there's Stirling Moss Limited – that's the holding company which controls all my own activities, together with Stirling Moss Enterprises Limited, which handles my Western Hemisphere involvements. Then there are other smaller companies, ranging from investments in things like jewellery and design. I'm a director of a company on design integration, which deals with anything from a car coat to a refrigerator, and I'm a director of Farr Ergonomics. . . .

'I'm also a director of Motor Racing Stables, at Brands Hatch – the racing driver school – and much of my time's taken up with PR involvements, giving advice and making appearances. I'm Director of Racing for Johnson Wax. Which means I made 28 visits to Canada and the US between June and November, 1970. I also do lecturing, vehicle evaluation for Chrysler (Australia), and occasional TV commentaries on US

races like Riverside. I do work for Opel on vehicle appraisal.
I've got the America Street Garage. I do work on flat design
and layout – making the best use of space, and so on. I'm
motoring editor of *Harper's, Queen* and *Penthouse,* and syndi-
cate newspaper articles each week, and I'm writing books – on
tape.

'I suppose the best way to describe me is "an international
prostitute !" '

I put a very obvious question : had you ever thought what
you'd do if you had such an accident? Straight back came
the frank reply : 'No. I was a very short-sighted, foolish man,
because I was racing until I was 32 with no thought or inten-
tion of retiring. I said I'd retire when other people were faster
than me through the corners. I was feeling fit, and my racing
was getting better. But I had no business whatever built up.
Racing's a full-time business, and unless one's intelligent
enough to do what I didn't do and set up a business, one's
left with nothing. One or two drivers, like Brabham and poor
Bruce McLaren, have been very wise in this respect.'
Financially, Moss is doing well in the business world, but he
calculates that he would be five times above his 1961 earnings
if he were still racing – in other words in the Jackie Stewart
£150,000-a-year-plus bracket.

Does he still think back and try to analyse that accident?
'I'm still interested in why and how it happened. But I'm
equally interested in what happened to Jimmy Clark, purely
because it's a point of great importance. In my case there was
no hint ... nothing. But I also think I tried myself out again
too soon afterwards. If I'd waited, I might have got back
into racing ...'

We talked for long about the current atmosphere of GP
racing, and Moss conceded that he had the feelings of an
old-timer. 'I suppose it's nostalgic to me – maybe it's a bit of
jealousy – but I think it's changed for the worse. The driving's
better; the cars are faster, tyre development is better, but to me
the sport itself isn't as good – the *passion* has gone.'

He recalled a 'passionate' incident, in 1951, when the great
Fangio, in trouble during a Grand Prix, smashed his fists into
the instrument panel, stormed out of the cockpit and let the
car roll down the track. 'You don't get that sort of feeling in

drivers now. The 'fifties were the passionate years. There's been a tremendous change. And I'm sorry. But it's the Collinses, Hawthorns and De Portagos who've gone. The characters are going ... Innes Ireland's a character, but he's no longer racing. Stewart is a character – but in a different sense. I think it's all a great shame. It used to be so much fun ... Imagine if they had the Mille Miglia now. Someone would ask for two thousand miles of guard rail.

'No, to my mind, the greatest hazard in racing is the man behind the wheel. Very few accidents are caused by mechanical failures. When they are, we invariably know.'

We met for our nostalgic talk at London's Café Royal – a place which incredibly, was unfamiliar to Moss. Typically, he burst through the revolving door into the plush foyer like a winner taking the flag, shedding car coat and fur deer-stalker as he came. 'Four minutes late, old man. Sorry! Just parked the scooter outside.' He had, too. For Moss moves fast. Taxis get in snarl-ups. But motor scooters move like Moss.

'Gee, man – just look at that decor! That was when they really went to town on ceilings,' he said as we dived into the ornate gilt and cherub-bedecked grill room. I wondered if retirement had slowed Moss down in any conceivable way. If it had, it wasn't obvious.

'No. I reckon my pace of life's speeded up. I fly at least 200,000 miles a year. Now the world's smaller and there are more races around. When I started racing in '49–50, we used to drive to the various races. There was very little flying done. So I think my life has speeded up purely because I am not forced to relax now. And I like it.'

Our talk turned to driving techniques, and the GP man's attitude. 'Someone the other day asked if I agreed that the correct way of driving is to win a race at the maximum speed,' said Moss. 'I said I'd rather lose a race driving fast enough to win, than win a race driving slow enough to lose. That's really my philosophy of racing.'

He saw only two ways of racing. 'You drive because you love racing, like to go fast, and like competition. Or you drive because you want to win. I needed to win.'

Was there anything he had learnt since his enforced retirement that might have changed his attitude to racing now? 'Yes. Looking back, I realise now that I should have driven for Ferrari. The year I retired, I had an offer from Ferrari. He was prepared to build me the car I wanted. But, I'd still want to be a "loner", because I enjoyed it that way. If I had a choice now, I'd want to choose a Brabham, or a McLaren probably, rather than go into a big team. But I still say Mercedes was the greatest team in the world. I loved it, and I had a fantastic year with them. But that's the way one should race. Again, I raced because I like to get in and drive. I was in the sport for the love of it.'

I recalled that, in his peak years, Moss had pitched his contracts pretty high. 'Sure,' he agreed. 'not because of the money I wanted, but because I wanted enough money to enable me to keep racing.' It was a fine point, but understandable.

Finally, we talked about the current breed of drivers, and the all-time greats. Moss listed his ten greats like this : 'Number one – unquestionably in GP racing, Fangio. The rest, not in any order, but including – Clark, Varzi, Caracciola, Nuvolari, Ascari, Wimille, Rosemeyer, Brooks, Stewart.' I raised an eyebrow at the name of Tony Brooks.

'Yes,' said Moss. 'In my mind one of the greatest drivers the world has ever known – who was never really known. He was an outstanding all-rounder.'

And the next World Champion? 'I think Regazzoni could be world champion in a year-and-a-half,' declared Moss. 'People like that come into racing and their performance just keeps going up. There are no peaks and falls. It's all consistent. He's the one I'd back.'

There is one old myth about Moss that I would like to dispel – the oft-quoted claim that he was an unsympathetic breaker of cars. One need only read *Design and Behaviour of the Racing Car*, which he wrote jointly with the late Laurence ('Pom') Pomeroy to appreciate that Moss's understanding and feeling for the machinery he drove went far deeper than most of his contemporaries were even capable of thinking – and that is no slight on their ability. Said Alf Francis, Moss's head mechanic for many years : 'It is uncanny how often Stirling is the driver who first experiences a particular weakness [in a car]. It is not that he thrashes cars, because I know, better than anyone else, that he does not.'

Jenkinson probably gets closer to the truth on this aspect when he talks of Moss's insistence on making 'unnecessary experiments' with his cars when he could beat all the opposition with a perfectly standard vehicle. Moss argued that only by continually experimenting with new ideas could one be prepared for any eventuality. Jenkinson puts Moss's lost championships down to mechanical misfortunes and bad mechanical judgment – choosing the wrong car or component.

'This,' Jenkinson contends, 'was because he was always seeking perfection and would not accept that he was perfection as a driver, which should have been sufficient. He tried to assist in design and preparation and the results were not as good as his driving.'

'Dedication' is the word that comes most readily to mind in one's attempts to analyse the Moss philosophy to living. Add in 'creativeness', 'flair' and 'artistry', and you have an instant cut-away picture of the man's talent bank.

Moss could almost certainly have switched his talent in any one of a dozen directions other than racing, and still become a world headliner – clothing design, jewellery design, interior décor, in fact any outlet in a creative-artistic field. His London house off Shepherd Market is a gadget-man's mecca. Its five storeys stand in the shadow of the Hilton Hotel, and it is automated from basement to roof. Moss has a control panel in his private office, duplicated in the master bedroom. The garage door operates on a sonic system. The kitchen is an ergonomic masterpiece. Rubbish disposal is mechanised. Curtains open and close under electronic power. Moss's toilet seat incorporates an electric warming circuit (with a warning light). Furnishing and décor are a melange of severe contemporary and discreet, solid Scandinavian. Ken Purdy, who devotes nearly a chapter to the Moss Home, observes : 'It's a portrait of him, almost : a small house, tightly put together, jumping with ideas, and burning almost enough energy every day to run a train from London to Manchester – and half-way back !'

It's certainly a house that you can only like or dislike. Sitting in the private office soon after Moss took command, I felt that he was probably watching my every reaction over the closed-circuit television, from his sunken, free-form bathtub . . . or the toilet seat.

Purdy, like Jenkinson and myself, was clearly fascinated by the dynamism and utter restlessness of Moss, and his superbly subtle appraisal of the man continually harks back to this aspect of his character. He draws Moss out on the thesis of driving as an art-form. 'Driving,' replies Moss, 'is a dance, in a way. And it's like skiing, too, very much like skiing . . . the same, but never the same, never monotonous . . . monotony in life would drive me mad. I can't bear inactivity; I get dis-heartened sometimes when I stop moving . . .'

I could never claim to have *understood* the complex character or mind of Moss, and would guess that no one else – apart from Moss himself – has succeeded in doing so. He could be described as good-humoured, witty, emotional, eloquent, deep-thinking, enterprising, creative, demonstrative, responsive, ebul-lient – certainly enigmatic. But we would still have only scratched the skin, for at the same time he can be polite, imperious, dominating, brusque, impatient, mercurial and im-petuous. I like him. Many of my colleagues find him com-pletely unapproachable – more, I believe, through their own impatience or failure to understand him. Again we come back to my original comparison with Winston Churchill. Who could truthfully claim ever to have *understood* him? When one thinks about it, probably every great character in history has been an enigma. Few of them have possessed any really close friends, though their acquaintances are numbered in scores.

Physically, Moss is small-built, lithe and very tough. Physical fitness has long been almost a fetish with him, and was no doubt the major contributing factor to his remarkable recovery after the accident. He moves like a dancer, his feet barely skimming the ground when he's pushed for time. Which is always. He has expressive hands, piercing eyes, and a ready smile. In a hackneyed phrase : 'he's my kind of man'.

# CHAPTER FOUR

# Jochen Rindt

## *by* Heinz Prüller

*Born Vienna 1921, Heinz Prüller started in journalism when he was thirteen and still at school. He started professionally in 1959 and is one of the most respected sporting writers in Europe. He is Sports Editor of Vienna Daily Express and has his own radio and television sports programmes. He was a close friend of Jochen Rindt which showed in an enthusiastic first broadcast from Le Mans in 1965 – when Rindt won. He has covered more than fifty Grands Prix, plus Indianapolis, and is the author of two best-selling books on Jochen Rindt.*

It was back in 1969 – November 14th. Jochen Rindt and I enjoyed a long evening in one of these typical wine-yards in the mountains surrounding Old Vienna. Jochen was drinking and smoking. He was no longer in his usual off-season mood from earlier years ('I just can't imagine how much effort it takes to drive in a Grand Prix when I am not sitting in a racing car for some weeks,' he used to say in the years 1965–67). He was sure of himself. He had won, at long last, his first Grand Prix – the American at Watkins Glen – something that had taken him 48 GP's, and he had organised a new Jochen Rindt Show.

'In 1970,' he told me, 'I want to be world champion and the biggest name in motor racing. But racing will only be a part of my life. When I have the title, I am going to retire immediately. I just don't want to be finished and exhausted before I am thirty and just carry on racing and racing because there is nothing else I want, can do – or am interested in. There are so many things which I would like to do. Time is the most valuable thing you can have. And listen : I will be

48

THAT VICTORY LOOK

Stirling Moss earning the cheers of a huge Silverstone crowd
as he takes his Cooper to Victory in July 1961.

## ANOTHER INCREDIBLE ESCAPE

Graham Hill was not the only driver to take flight in the grim 1969 Grand Prix (see pictures facing page 32).

It happened to Jochen Rindt's car too—and big wings were banned as a result.

living another, say, fifty years. But I have taken out from twenty-eight years more than you can usually gain. Isn't that simple to understand?'

It was. But I asked him: 'All right, you get the title. But then, wouldn't you like the idea of becoming one of the all-time greats, maybe equalling Jimmy Clark's world record of twenty-five GP wins?'

'Look where Jimmy is,' he answered slowly.

'And the one GP win, at least a tremendous effort, is not enough?'

'No, because I have to prove something.'

'That you are the best in the world?'

'Yes. Because today there are only two real top professionals: Jackie Stewart and myself. Because we drive with our heads.'

He was possibly the most intelligent driver of his era. He could calculate the risks. 'The possibility of getting killed,' he said, 'is a big one. It's just luck, good luck or bad luck, whether you can manage to survive. I have been racing for eight years now, no one can understand what it means: eight years of racing!'

He kept on drinking and smoking, he lowered his voice: 'My show alone can earn me my living.' His plans for retiring after 1970, which he told me as a secret, were seriously meant. How seriously, I learnt the day after, when Nina told me: 'Jochen promised to pay me £10,000 if he wins the Championship and doesn't give up racing.' Something that really indicates how Jochen thought. He would never give £10,000 ($24,000) away!

Everything was set up for his ambition – 'Jochen Rindt for world Champion.' He had arranged with Colin Chapman, after a rather tumultous beginning of their association, that he was to drive the new Lotus 72 which was to be a world-beater. Lotus had officially announced that they were to make an all-out effort in Formula One, cancelling the Indianapolis – and the Can Am projects.

How well it worked out Jochen, tragically, was never to know. He was killed at Monza in the last practice session, at 3.35 Italian summertime, the same time as his great friend Piers Courage at Zandvoort. But the forty-five points he had managed in the first eight out of thirteen races were to be unequalled by any other driver. Therefore Jochen became the first German-speaking world champion, the twelfth in the list of the big names. Of them, seven are still alive, and Jochen was the only one to be killed in a Formula One car. He was the sport's first posthumous champion.

'The more success he had, the nicer he became,' Rob Walker wrote in his Austrian Grand Prix report for an American magazine – three weeks before Monza. And this Austrian GP at, the new, modern 'Österreichring', only two miles from the bumpy airfield circuit on which Walker had given Jochen his first Formula One drive in 1964, indicated only too well, how Jochen had developed. 100,000 people came to cheer and support him. When he dropped out after only twenty-one laps because of engine trouble, the crowd started to leave the circuit. Those who stayed cheered him as a National hero – something that he had really become. The whole national industry, the whole national way of life seemed to be built around him. Jochen was seemingly the centre of everything. He very seldom showed how proud he was of what he had achieved. At Zeltweg, Jochen did not hide it.

In his youth, Jochen Rindt was tough, ruthless, fearless and competitive. He was not an easy boy to handle. His parents, who owned a pepper and spice grinding mill in Mainz, Germany, were killed in a bombing raid in 1943 when Jochen was only fifteen months old. He was brought up by his grandparents in Graz. His grandfather, a lawyer, had a lot of trouble coping with the police fines that Jochen collected for speeding on his motor cycle.

Jochen and his school friends – Helmut Marko was one – were known as the 'horrifying four' and they took to driving cars long before they were eighteen. They organised races on public roads, stopping the traffic by telling the other motorists that – 'This is an official test drive.' When they were out driving they would change places at the wheel if the other three thought that the driver had not taken a bend at 'ten-tenths'.

Jochen changed schools several times, and at one stage his grandparents sent him to Chichester to learn English. (In fact he spent most of his time sailing). So it is not true, as some

English journalists think, that the first English words Jochen learnt were 'starting money'.

At school, Jochen was always the one who did the organising. He was the best tennis player and skier of his school, but broke his leg twice when skiing, the second time on the day before he was to pass his driving test. 'The James Dean films,' he once said, 'were simple fairy tales compared with what we did.'

He took up racing for fun. He started in an old Simca which his grandparents had bought for him, and later he drove an Alfa Giulietta tuned at Conreros with which he blew off all the Italian Champions in their hill climbs. 1963 saw his Formula Junior season in an old Cooper, bought by Kurt Barry (who was to be killed in a road accident in February of 1964). '1964 was the year I needed all the angels to protect me,' Jochen said, and when asked how often he had driven beyond his limits, he answered calmly : 'Did I ever drive within my limits in those days?'

He won pole position in his first Formula Junior race at Vallelunga in heavy rain. He won his second Formula Junior race at Cesenatico, beating Italian ace Geki Russo. He fought, he crashed and he managed good places in an already one-year-old car. He crashed at the Nürburgring when he was blocked by a slow car – at the medical check in the hospital he said : 'I had better give up racing, I am too nervous for this business.' But later he decided : 'I found out that there is nothing I can do better than drive a racing car. And this makes me happy, because otherwise I would have had wasted two years. Now I am going to make a profession out of it and I will do everything to climb to the top.'

The £4,000 ($9,600) that the twenty-two-year-old Jochen spent (from the spice mill money) to buy a Formula Two Brabham for 1964 was to be as Jochen put it, 'a good investment, I guess'. He came to England for the White races, asking Denny Hulme if he would be allowed to follow him for some laps to learn the circuit of Mallory Park – he ended up with pole position ! Though his clutch gave trouble at the start, Jochen worked his way through the field and came third. The day after, Graham Hill, at Crystal Palace, asked his mechanics : 'Who is the boy alongside me on the front row?' 'Jochen Rindt of

Austria,' they told him. 'Never heard of him,' Graham answered, 'is he a skier?'

Jackie Stewart, the rising Formula Three star and actually the only new face those days, looked at Jochen and described his feelings to me : 'He looks like a boy, his helmet doesn't seem to fit, he looks slightly out of place, and he looks like a loner : Somebody who doesn't want to need help and doesn't want the others to believe that he needs help.' In the fifteenth lap of the forty lap race Jochen fought his way past Hill – and won! 'Unknown Australian,' one London newspaper told its readers next morning, 'beats Hill.' The day after, Dennis Druitt from BP altered Jochen's original contracts – £25 ($60) per race, £1,200 ($2,880) for the season – and a delighted Jochen told me : 'It feels like dreaming.'

He learnt how to forget dreadful accidents during a race (in Rheims, he drove straight into his pit after he had seen the Arundell crash just in front of him, and gave up), and he kept on studying the big names : 'Jimmy Clark looks more often in the mirrors than everybody else, I feel always very safe when I am near to him. The same goes for Graham Hill, though he is fighting wheel to wheel, but he would never put me in an embarrassing situation. He is driving very tough, but I am not different to him in that matter.' His constantly quick driving led to a Formula One contract. I went with Jochen to the London Racing Car Show in January 1965 when he signed his three-year contract with Coopers. 'Three years is maybe too long, but I don't have much other choice.' He got on quite well with his team-mate Bruce McLaren. 'We didn't become great friends, we didn't come close to each other, but I don't think that we wanted to. It happens in every team that number one and number two are not such big friends.' Jochen fought with all sorts of technical troubles, came fourth at Nürburgring and sixth at Watkins Glen which made four points, not a bad beginning, though he was overshadowed by Jackie Stewart's fantastic rise to prominence. 'In the Formula Two races,' I mentioned at Monza when Jackie won and Jochen came a disappointing eighth, 'you are usually ahead of Jackie.' Jochen smiled : 'That's because Jackie is driving a Cooper in Formula Two!'

Earning £2,000 ($4,800) for his first Formula. One year and

£200 ($480) per race, he was a cheap driver for Cooper. Look-
ing at Jochen's three years with the Surbiton team generally, the
atmosphere in the team was not always what he might have
wished. Roy Salvadori, then the Cooper race manager, seemed to
be somewhat hard on Jochen. And there was Jochen : desperately trying to establish himself. It was a clash of characters, or,
as Rob Walker felt : 'One solid fight.' During this Cooper period,
I remember Jochen saying to Salvadori : 'I can change my team
much easier than you can,' or, at Monte Carlo : 'Would you
like to drive instead of me?' Once in Monza he complained, his
voice, half Tom Sawyer, half Peter Pan : 'Roy, why do our cars
never look like real racing cars?'

Fate always seemed to favour the other driver – in 1966
Richie Ginther, then John Surtees, and in 1967 Pedro
Rodriguez. Jochen kept on fighting and trying. He put the
Cooper Maserati (overweight and underpowered) in horrifying
angles to keep up with the leaders, 'but this was my only
chance with this car.' Nevertheless, he did enormous drives.
No one will ever forget Jochen's fantastic performance in the
1966 Belgian Grand Prix, the race with the near-catastrophic
first lap which eliminated eight cars and in which Jochen was
leading from the fourth to the twenty-fourth lap only to be
beaten by Surtees (in John's last race for Ferrari) because of
differential or tyre troubles. Jochen came fourth in Rheims,
nursing an overcooking engine home in dreadful heat, losing
ten pounds in weight and thinking 'at least ten times of retiring',
he came fifth at Brands Hatch, fourth at Monza and second
at Watkins Glen, finishing the year with a third place in the
Championship behind Brabham and Surtees.

'I think, I always managed the maximum with the car,'
Jochen said, suggesting that drivers should not only be rated
by their results but also by what they are getting out of their cars.
His last Cooper year, 1967, earned him £10,000 ($24,000) salary,
but disappointment after disappointment, only managing fourth
places at Spa and Monza. At Watkins Glen, he was walking
back to the Cooper pit for the last time. 'This damned engine
broke again so I gave it an extra kick up to 12,000 revs to
make sure,' he told his mechanic, not realising that Salvadori
was standing just behind him. The Maserati engine was, at
that stage of the race ready to break anyway, but this story is

an exception. Jochen was not the car- or the engine-killer that some people thought he was. No one ever realized how much Jochen suffered because of this undeserved reputation that his many retirements had given to him. When other drivers packed up, everybody investigated the reason for it. When Jochen dropped out, they usually did not look for the cause. It had to be Jochen who had 'murdered' the car. And Jochen desperately tried to prove people wrong.

Some of these wrong-impressions go back to his early years, for instance Le Mans. Jochen was sharing a Chinetti-Ferrari LM with Masten Gregory in the twenty-four hour race in 1965. They gave the car starting number twenty-one – the same that Jochen had had for his first Formula Junior win (Cesenatico) and for his first Formula Two win (Crystal Palace). Jochen did not think of it when the Ferrari dropped back near to the end of the field with all sorts of mechanical bothers before darkness. The Chinetti pit wanted to retire the car, because they thought that the valves were broken. Gregory tried to prove to them that there was only a change of the condensator necessary. By the time this was done, it was Jochen's turn to take over. Gregory found Jochen behind the pits, already changed, ready to drive home the whole way to Vienna. 'Because there is no chance to win,' Jochen said. Gregory said : 'Are you crazy? There is no way to lose . . . if we carry on.' Jochen agreed with his American partner : 'All right, but from now on we are driving Grand Prix-style, flat out all the way. Either we are going to break the car or we are going to win. There is no other possibility.' So the flag fell for the 'twenty hour Grand Prix of Le Mans.' Needless to say, Jochen won, driving absolutely on the limit, gaining the lead for 200 yards at four in the morning, losing it, regaining it before noon when he ignored all team orders given by the then Ferrari team manager Dragoni, who desperately tried to convince the Ferrari-privateers that they should not fight against each other. From two to four it should have been Jochen's turn, but Gregory asked him : 'May I take the flag? I have waited for this for ten years, but you will win Le Mans several times.' Jochen agreed, and Masten nursed the car home with a sick differential, cutting out the engine before the curves. When it was all over and a mechanic drove the car back to the paddock, the differential finally broke after 200 yards ... !

It is sad to note that on September 5th, when the shock news from Monza arrived, Gregory again was at Le Mans, again driving a Chinetti-Ferrari, but for the Steve McQueen film.

Jochen was not going to race sports cars for ever. He did not get much pleasure out of driving to team orders. He also stopped his saloon car racing (in 1966 he helped Alfa to win the European Championship). He concentrated on Formula One and Formula Two, the Formula which you could call 'Formula Rindt', because there was never anybody who dominated this Formula in the way Rindt did, though Jacky Ickx quite rightly commented : 'To say that Jochen was the King of Formula Two is to insult him, because that could indicate that there is no place for him on a higher platform.' He won twenty-nine races in Formula Two. He beat Jimmy Clark in Rheims in 1965, when everybody said : 'To stay ahead of Jimmy for a few laps is sensational enough.' He beat the 'unbeatable' Brabham-Hondas of Jack and Denny at Brands Hatch in 1966, after having worked out during the whole season that this would be possible. Maybe he would have stopped racing altogether after 1967, the year he was having problems at Coopers, if he had not shown, in Formula Two, how good he was. He won nine races in 1967 and would have totalled 107 points (according to the Formula One system). He beat Jimmy on several occasions, and he did the same to Jackie.

'The best race I ever did before Monaco 1970, was the Zolder Formula Two race in 1968,' Jochen once told me. He had won the first heat comfortably, but at the start of the second heat was pushed from behind by Brian Redman, spun backwards through the whole field, that was already moving, surprisingly without hitting anything, and then started to attack. 'There are a lot of good drivers these days,' Stirling Moss once told me, 'but there are very few that can bring out the tiger in them when their odds are down, but Jochen is able to.' At Zolder, Jochen won after a sensational drive. In later years, he always thought about Zolder : 'I must have a Zolder race at the beginning of every season : A race that proves to me that I can manage to win even when things go wrong. I need that to be sure of myself and to be on top form.'

His string of Formula Two successes in the Winkelman-Brabham led to a Brabham Formula One contract in 1968. 'I like the Brabham car, it suits my style,' Jochen said, after having turned down offers from every team (except Lotus). 'I don't think I am going to become rich with Brabhams, but Jack provides me with a motor car I can win the world championship with, and this is much more worthwhile to me than everything else.' Jochen felt very safe with Brabhams. 'Every time I climbed in his car was like Christmas. With Jack, I always have the impression that he is driving the same car as I do, and therefore Jack gives all safety problems more thought than other constructors do.' He felt he was protected, and it was important for him to be under Jack's wing. He was no longer the 'daredevil driver' who was risking everything. 'You have to risk everything to climb up to the top. But once you are almost there, your experience does a lot for you. To drive beyond your limits doesn't necessarily make you go faster.' Without any doubt, Jochen was already champion material in 1968. He had learned to 'read a race', he had improved his technical knowledge considerably, he was able to set up a car much faster than before, obviously the association with Jack in whom he had 100 per cent confidence did a lot for him. Jochen admired Brabham: 'Fantastic, how casual, how unaffected, how modest Jack is.' This was something Jochen wanted to be himself. He admired how much Jack was able to take out from life. But he also admired Jimmy Clark even more. 'Jimmy was my best friend in the racing world, as far as you can be a friend, with a fellow driver,' Jochen said. When Jimmy was killed at Hockenheim, Jochen was sitting in the pits of Brands Hatch (100 km race). He was stunned when he heard the news.

'No one leaves the road in a gentle corner that is almost a straight,' Jochen told me, 'not even at 250 miles an hour in the wet, and Jimmy, who never made a mistake, is the last man who could do so. I am sure he was not killed because of a driver's error.

What happened, I don't know. Why it happened, I don't

know either. But it's always the same: whether Formula One, Formula Two or Indy, if somebody makes a mistake, the result is the same. And this gives me a lot of thoughts.'

It was possibly the first time that Jochen tried to analyse a fatal accident. As far as the Bandini accident in Monaco 1967 is concerned, Jochen put it down to a driver's mistake. 'Bandini exhausted himself during the race, he got tired.' The day Bandini died (three days after the accident), Jochen himself had his horrifying Indianapolis accident. Typically Jochen had worked out before what to do in case he should run into any trouble: 'I must avoid frontal impact with the barrier, I must force the car into a spin and hit the wall at an angle.' When the throttle of his Eagle jammed, Jochen managed to spin the car and he hit the wall at a small angle. Both right side wheels were knocked off and the car caught fire. Jochen controlled this accident (it happened at more than 200 miles an hour) calmly. He stayed in his seat and jumped out only when he had reduced the speed to about twenty miles an hour. The ambulance drove him to the hospital. When the main door was closed, Jochen left his stretcher, climbed out, opened the door, closed it, sat beside the driver and even offered him a cigarette. It took him three days to realize how dangerous this accident had been. 'At Indy,' Jochen told me the night before the race in a local steak house, 'Every European driver must feel like he is on the way to his own funeral. Indy does really interest me. If it had not been for the money, I would have never come. It's ridiculous and it's highly dangerous.'

Before the start, when they played the *Stars and Stripes* and when Eddy Fisher sang *Back Home Again In Indiana*, Jochen asked me from the car: 'Which sort of day is it – the memorial day?' The memorial day for soldiers, I said, 'Favourable day, today,' Jochen said slowly.

It was there in Indianapolis, where Mike Spence was killed, and in 1968 Scarfiotti and Schlesser also lost their lives. The season was overshadowed. Jochen tried terribly, terribly hard to win his first GP, but he had to be content with two pole positions (Rouen and Canada) and two thirds (South Africa and Nürburgring). The four cam Repco engine always let him down, and Jack refused a mid-season offer from Ford to change to the fast and reliable Cosworth engine, because of his loyalty to Repco. But Jochen and Jack never had the slightest argument : 'We were hopeful all the time and convinced that everything must work out in the next race.' But it never did. Jochen was never under any pressure from the team, but there were other things that gave him a lot of thought.

There was the McLaren car that carried Denny and Bruce to three GP wins in 1968 and to fifty-five championship points together. It was the same car that was originally designed for Jochen and the Winkelmann-Team, but BP dropping out and Firestone's drastic reduction of sponsor money finished the project.

There were the aerofoils – something that made Jochen suspicious all the time. When he came to Monza, (1968), he was really alarmed : 'I was in an aerodynamic expert's office in Paris,' he said, 'these wings are really dangerous. They told me when the wing is going to break the whole car reacts like an aeroplane and gets air-borne.' The wings started in Spa in 1968, but they grew and grew and it seemed to become a sort of competition which team had the bigger wings.

In Monza practice 1968 Jochen lost a wheel at the parabolica but without running into any troubles. 'The same thing can happen to me at Lotus,' he told me, 'but Lotus pays me more money.' In fact, Colin Chapman had approached Jochen at Brands Hatch during the British Grand Prix. Jochen asked for a lot of money. Colin came back from the sponsors and said that they had agreed. Jochen did not really want to join Lotus. He tried to get into the four wheel drive Cosworth car designed by Robin Herd, he also was offered the same deal that Stewart had in '68 and '69 : free Matra-Chassis, Ford, Dunlop. In both cases it would have been Winkelmann's problem to pay Rindt, but Alan Rees had a lot of problems to raise the sponsorship money.

Jochen felt that he could easily win the World Championship. 'All I need is the right car and a little bit of luck, though it does not necessarily indicate that you are the best driver in the world when you are the World Champion.' When I asked whether he thought that Jackie Stewart had taken over Jim Clark's role in GP racing, he said : 'That's your opinion.' But he said during the wet summer of '68 : 'Another rain race and Jackie has it.' Jackie did not get it. Jochen hesitated to join Lotus. 'If I should leave Brabham, I would only do it with a broken heart. Jack, Ron (Tauranac) and Leo (Mehl) are the nicest chaps in motor racing.' Brabham tried to raise sponsorship to keep Jochen in the team, but whatever money he came up with, it was only half of what Chapman offered. Jochen felt that he had stuck out his neck long enough for comparatively small money. He felt that he had to have a competitive car. Finally, it was all decided in Mexico City.

We had a long dinner at the Richelieu restaurant. Jochen told me that he had decided for Lotus. When we walked home the night before the GP Jochen explained to me : 'I can't afford it to stay with Brabham and gave away half the money. Lotus is going to be my third team now. One should not change too much, but if success doesn't come soon, I could be finished.' He seemed to be very confident: 'Lotus produces the best car, the biggest sensations, there is nothing that Chapman can't realize technicalwise. To be really competitive, there is not the smallest problem.' 'Human problems?' I asked. 'That's the biggest problem. Chapman is a cool businessman, and Hill is the champ. But I am not number two.' A few days later, Jochen surprised Colin by saying : 'In case I win the title this year, don't expect great speeches. I will go home to Geneva immediately.' 'But why?' asked Colin. 'It's part of the championship to give speeches ... but we can discuss this problem later in the season.'

The Rindt-Lotus association did not start too encouragingly. Jochen crashed in Levin (Tasman race) at the Eifelpokal Formula Two race (Nürburgring) the wishbone broke. Before the Spanish GP at Barcelona Jochen was sent as the GPDA representative to check the safety of the Montjuich circuit. He found the guard rails much too low, they looked as if a car could easily jump over. 'We have got the measurements from the Monza director,' the Spaniards told him ... Jochen suggested alterations, and they promised to do them. In the race Jochen was pulling away from the second man, Chris Amon, almost a second a lap, in fact he was leading his first GP since the rain race at Spa, in 1966, when his wing broke on lap nineteen, in a slight left turn. He was travelling at 150 miles an hour on the very same spot that his

59

team-mate Graham Hill had crashed at ten laps earlier. What happened was exactly what Jochen was frightened of. The car turned left, went airborne, climbed up the guard-rail, came back, turned right, crashed into Graham's Lotus and turned over. Jochen was half-conscious when they took him out, he had a broken nose and facial injuries. He was brought to Soler-Roigs clinic (Alex' father). His wife Nina, his friend Bernie Ecclestone and I were the first ones to be allowed into Jochen's room. 'Did you get my starting money?' Jochen asked Bernie, and when Stewart, who felt as if he had stolen the race, heard about this, he smiled for the first time that day : 'Bloody Jochen doesn't change . . .'

Next day in the hospital, Jochen said, half asleep : 'I always wanted to know how Jimmy felt, I think I know it now : nothing, absolutely nothing. You watch what is going on from a neutral position, as if somebody else is going to crash. Without the double guard-rails, there would be now two Grand Prix drivers less : Graham and myself.'

He could not race at Monaco, when Graham won, he watched the race on TV and said : 'I think I am the catastrophy Charlie from every team. I am always in the wrong cars in the wrong races at the wrong time.' He found out in those days about Colin : 'His character is very complicated to describe. Obviously he wants to win, but the way he wants to win and I want to win are different, that's probably the reason for arguments.' Chapman told me his feelings about Jochen : 'He made it very difficult for me to get to know him, it took me almost a year. But once I knew him I discovered that he had a heart of gold. He is so very, very blunt, but sincere and honest in all his opinions.' But before Chapman found out, there were a lot of arguments. Jochen refused for a very long time to try the four-wheel-drive Lotus 63. A driver who said 'no' was a completely new situation for Colin who mentioned that he had never had 'a more complicated driver'.

Nevertheless, Jochen won his comeback race after the accident (Zolder, Formula Two), he was leading the Dutch Grand Prix before dropping out because of technical failure, he retired in the very hot French Grand Prix because of physical sickness — 'I always had Bandini in front of me, I was frightened that I would kill myself. Bandini got sick during the Monaco race, I was already sick at the start.' In fact, he always hated racing in hot weather. He had his monumental battle with Stewart in the British Grand Prix, leading from the start to the sixth lap and again from the sixteenth to the sixty-first lap only to become a dreadfully disappointed fourth because of two pit stops – one to get a loose part of his aerofoil fixed and one to pick up some more fuel.

Silverstone, this great battle, was to tell the story of the year '69 : 'Jackie didn't only win his races, but he also won my races,' Jochen said. Still without a GP win, was it ever going to come? The arguments in the Lotus camp were not finished at all. Jochen was locked up with his March project, they had already finished some advertising booklets, and a newspaper had done a big story on Jochen, entitled : 'Is this man the perfect racing driver?' Chapman took him into the Lotus caravan during the Nürburgring practice. 'Don't believe this, Jochen! You are far away from being a perfect racing driver. You are fine in the car, but you are a bastard out of it.' Nevertheless, Colin offered Jochen an all-out effort for the title in 1970, including concentration on only one, his, car – the Jim Clark service. We drove to a Lotus party down to a small Mosel village. Colin was nice, served champagne, Jochen was nice and I told him : 'Look, Jochen, in a few years you will say : "I had a lot of arguments with Chapman, but we finally finished them, agreed on a fruitful association and it paid off!" ' Jochen looked surprised : 'Me staying with Lotus? No, impossible.'

The odds went better now. Jochen lost the Monza race to Jackie Stewart by only a few inches. He came third in Canada, beaten by his tyres. But then, at long last, he won the United States Grand Prix Watkins Glen, and was delighted about his friend Courage coming second. He could not believe that he was going to win till the last lap, 'and even then I was not sure what was going to break in the last few yards.' He was surprised that he did not feel too much happiness, 'because I have waited for this too long.' He had tried forty-eight GP's to win one, and when he succeeded, he could not understand what had made it so difficult. But his day of triumph was overshadowed : Team-mate Graham Hill had crashed quite seriously.

This was the situation in which Jochen found himself before his year of glory and disaster. Jochen Rindt – the complete European : Born in Germany, brought up in Austria, driving for a British team, living in Switzerland, married to a half-Swedish, half-Russian Finnish girl. Nina is from a very sporting family : her father, Kurt Lincoln, is a successful Finnish sports car and Formula Junior driver, her mother plays bridge for the Finnish National team and her brother competed in the Wimbledon Junior Tennis Tournament. Jochen knew Nina from his Formula Junior days back in 1963 and they married in 1967 before the season started. They had a baby, named Natascha Jonin (Jochen+Nina) in August 1968, a few days after the foggy Nürburgring race. They first lived in Paris, but in 1969 Jochen decided to move out of Paris 'because the traffic is horrible, the telephoning complicated and there is never any parking place at the airport.' They went to Begnins, where Jackie Stewart found them a rented house before their own house (worth £100,000 – $240,000) was built on land bought from Bonnier. Jochen continued to be a courageous and skilled skier, loving racing in the deep snow. He passed his motorboat licence test after only two hours of learning, he seemed to enjoy life more from day to day. His Jochen Rindt Show (he had started it with a £10,000 ($24,000) investment in 1965) grew from year to year. It was already the biggest on the Continent. Jochen planned every extra detail including organising Rolls Royces for his guest stars in Vienna, Walter Hayes, Jackie Stewart, Bob Martin, Leo Mehl, etc. More and more, he was a tremendous ambassador for Austria.

Sometimes, it looked as if Formula One racing was the least important thing for Jochen. He organised his show perfectly, he found pleasure in his own Formula Two team and he wanted to become World Champion – maybe in that order. The dream of his own team finally came true. With the Formula Two team offer Chapman had beaten Jack Brabham who wanted desperately to get Jochen back for 1970 (and, in fact, thought for some weeks in late summer that all was agreed. In that case Jack would have retired from racing before 1970!) Jochen built up the Formula Two team together with his great English friend Bernie Ecclestone. They even had their own aeroplane – a Beagle, something that gave me unforgettable hours high up in the clouds with Jochen flying the aeroplane after only a few lessons and still far away from his pilot's licence. Once we crossed Mainz in Germany: 'This is my birth town,' Jochen said excited, 'and there is my factory.' The aeroplane and the factory – Jochen gave the impression of Jonas Cord, the wild young one in Robbins' *The Carpetbaggers*. But he added: 'This aeroplane is only for multimillionaires. I won't be able to afford it in 1971 after I have retired from racing.' And he was not that wild any more – he was mellow, relaxed, somebody you simply had to like.

The story of Jochen Rindt, his 1970 season and the Lotus 72 is in the history books now. At first, the new 'wonder car' made him slightly suspicious. In Madrid, he had his practice accident because the insulating material next to the inboard front disc brakes had melted and loosened the bolts. Fortunately, he did not hit anything.

For Monaco, he went back to the old, faithful 49. His practice times were far from encouraging, but the whole set-up of the car was changed the night before the race. No chance to win, Jochen felt, on race day. Bernie told him: 'What ever happens, don't come back to the pits today, except walking.' Colin said: 'You always have a chance in racing, put on the pressure, carry on, you don't have to win races from the lead, especially at Monaco.' The first half of the race Jochen drove, according to his words, 'like a cab driver'. But then, suddenly, the dynamo in Jochen started to work, something that made him drive like a devil. His Monaco performance alone should indicate that Jochen in 1969 and 1970 was as fast as Jimmy was, maybe faster – but it would have taken more time to prove than Jochen was given in his short, hot summer of glory.

At Monaco, he passed Pescarolo, Hulme and found himself with fifteen laps to go fifteen seconds behind the leading Brabham. He caught Jack rapidly. Jochen was one of those drivers who never can understand why millions are thrilled by watching races – 'I find motor racing rather boring, but in Monaco for the first time I got excited.' He drove Brabham, the old fox, into a braking error in the last bend, the Gasometer, and won the best race of his life. He could not believe that he had won. Jochen never cared too much about publicity.

But about the fantastic Monaco press stories he really got a little bit romantic.

A few days later, Bruce McLaren was killed. Nina told Jochen when she picked him up at Geneva airport, and Jochen could not believe it. 'That it happened to Bruce, who was probably the last man to have an accident, indicates that this can happen to everyone.'

Then came Spa, the circuit that Jochen said was too frightening at any speed and in any weather. During practice, Jochen's back suspension collapsed.

For Zandvoort, the car was made stronger. He scored his first Lotus 72 win and his third Grand Prix win, but did not get the slightest joy because Piers Courage was killed in the early stages of the race, and Jochen knew it. 'I saw the burning car and I saw Piers' helmet very near to the car. For some laps I desperately hoped that he had climbed out and taken away his helmet, but then I realised that Piers, if he had come out, would never put his helmet down so near to the car.' Nina left with Sally, not knowing that Jochen had won, and on the way to the airport Jochen discussed with Bernie whether he should retire immediately, but then Jochen decided : 'You have to finish what you have started, you can't drop out half-way through a season.' 'Servoz-Gavin could,' Nina said, but Jochen refused : 'If I want to keep my self-respect, I can't quit during the season.'

At Piers' funeral, Jochen was – for the first time in his life – in tears. He remembered the happy winter weeks he, Piers, Sally, Nina and an Austrian friend of theirs had had in the Austrian Alps skiing. A few weeks later, the Austrian friend died from cancer. 'What do you think is better?' a dispirited Jochen asked Nina, 'Dying like Ernst (the Austrian) or dying like Piers?' He helped poor Sally as much as he could and he and Nina spent more time with Sally than Chapman would have liked. 'But, once again, that proves how sincere he was. He felt more for Piers and Sally than for racing.'

He also won the next Grand Prix, the French one, on the Clermont-circuit that he did not like at all. He played his cards coolly, waiting until the front runners, Beltoise and Ickx ran into trouble and then won the race from third place, holding off attacks from Amon. For the first time, he was

leading the Drivers Championship. 'If it had happened the
year before, I would have been the happiest man in the world.
But two weeks after Piers' death, it just doesn't matter that
much,' he told me the evening after the race. 'But I want to
do everything possible to win the Championship this year, and
that means that I will be content at some races with second
or third places, just to collect points.' Chapman did not quite
understand : 'Why second or third, Jochen? We are going to
win every race !'

By now, he was absolutely confident in the car, the inboard
disc brakes did not worry him any more. At the first day of
Grand Prix training at Brands Hatch, he gave Chapman the
nicest words he probably ever said to him : 'Absolutely perfect!
Don't touch the car, don't alter anything, it's bloody marvellous.' Tyre problems in the race prevented Jochen from staying
ahead of an attacking Brabham with only twelve laps to go.
Jack went by and opened a gap. Jochen, content to come
second, found himself winning after Jack ran out of petrol in
the last lap. 'My luck now really starts worrying me,' he
admitted in the Lotus caravan where I met him in the same
position he always was after a race – behind the steering wheel,
the window half open, signing autographs, handing them back,
like a post office clerk. 'I know how fast good luck can turn
back on you, bringing bad luck with it. And I have had some
good fortune during this summer.'

He gave the questions of security more thoughts than ever
before. He did not want to race at Oulton Park for that reason,
but Chapman wanted him to do so. He refused an offer to drive
in the Zeltweg 1000 km championship race, 'because you never
know : Maybe bad luck comes just at this race?' He was the
GPDA representative for the Nürburgring and he was quite
outspoken about security problems : 'You can't make the cars
slower, so you have to make the circuits safer. Motor racing
does not gain reputation from the accidents, no one comes and
pays to see somebody killed. But if something happens, whether
an oil leak or some breakage of the car, there must be something safer than trees.' Sometime in this summer he said to
Nina – 'In three year's time racing will be a hundred per cent
safe, at least as far as the racing tracks are concerned.'

The race was held at the Hockenheim circuit. Jochen was

involved in a heroic battle against the Ferraris of Ickx and Regazzoni, he gained a lot of respect for Ickx's fair, clean driving on that day, and he won. It was his sixth and last Grand Prix garland. His mechanics laid it on the spot in the back straight where Jimmy Clark had been killed twenty-eight months previously. They had already started to toast Jochen as a new Jim Clark, but Jochen seemed to be rather bored after the most convincing of his Grand Prix victories. 'A monkey would have won with your car today,' he smiled to Chapman, and on the winners rostrum he immediately took up business talks with von Hanstein about his racing car show in Germany.

Because of the Lotus turbine car and some sensational business offers he now decided to carry on racing for another year, 'and we will see what happens by then'. He was on the top of his life, everything went as he wanted it, he was happy and at peace with everything when he took out his BMW, one of his three cars, to drive to Monza.

He managed only the sixth best time in Friday practice. But overnight he got a new Cosworth engine, and the gear ratios were set two cogs higher. The speed diagram of the so-geared DG 300 gearbox gives a 205 miles an hour top speed.

On Saturday morning Jochen wanted to work on our book about his way to the Championship, but I thought a longer sleep would do much more good for him – and I felt a little bit superstitious about starting to work on a book about the Championship before Jochen had actually won the title.

Jochen once described to me his feeling of going through a bend like a 'stone rotating on a rope'. At the Parabolica, the rope was cut when Jochen started braking.

At 28 years of age, Jochen Rindt was lost to racing. Killed when only hours after his accident he could have been receiving the World's acclaim as the new Champion.

Somehow the rest of the season didn't seem to matter. Piers Courage, Bruce McLaren and now Jochen. No season was worth such a terrible price. Jochen's death made it statistically possible for any of five drivers – Stewart, Brabham, Hulme, Regazzoni or Ickx – to claim the title if they had a continuous run of success in the remaining races. It may sound trite and emotional – but nobody wanted it to happen.

It would be the final cruelty if Jochen were to be robbed of his title after his magnificent Monaco, Dutch, French, British and German victories. Jacky Ickx won in Canada and Mexico – but a pit stop in the US Grand Prix which dropped him to fourth place guaranteed that justice was done. Jochen Rindt became motor racing's first postumous World Champion.

His wife Nina – whose courage inspired everyone who met her during those terrible weeks after Jochen's death – wrote to Jacky Ickx as follows :

'First of all, I want to congratulate you on your win in Canada. To be honest : I was a little worried that you might win Watkins Glen and Mexico City as well, which would have meant that Jochen had lost the Championship. I am very happy that Jochen managed it after all : it was his only burning wish.'

It was a wish fulfilled in one of those stranger-than-fiction episodes that seem continually to colour motor racing. Jochen Rindt's successor in the Lotus team – young Brazilian Emerson Fittipaldi – won his first Grand Prix at Watkins Glen. And ensured that his late team-mate would take the title. Honour was satisfied. And Team Lotus had paid their own tribute to their lost leader.

Jacky Ickx, the sensitive Belgian who genuinely didn't seem to mind missing the 1970 Championship, put into words what many of us wanted to feel.

He wrote : 'I consider it important that Jochen Rindt died a happy man. When, after four years of courage and disappointment, success in Grand Prix racing finally came to him, he became a different person. At the moment when he climbed into his car for the last time, he was particularly happy. He had the looks and manners of a contented man.

'There can be little doubt that he remained happy until the very moment of his accident, for we drivers are always happy behind the wheel.

'And even if one can talk of an untimely death, all I can say is that the duration of life should not be measured in days or hours, but by that which we achieve during the time given to us. There isn't a single one of us who hasn't left his hotel room in the morning well aware that he may not return, but this does not prevent us from achieving complete happiness.

'On the contrary, perhaps it enables us to be all the more so.

The knowledge that everything could finish before the end of the day enables us to enjoy the wonders of life and all that surrounds it all the more.'

Perhaps then it is we who are left behind who are the poorer. And the whole Austrian nation joined in the mourning when the motor-racing world came to Graz to pay their respects. There were 32 planes at the small airport and 30,000 people came to say farewell to Jochen : the man who wanted to quit racing before he was thirty : who wanted to grow old because he had so many other interests in life.

The boy who was so much more than just a racing driver, the boy for whom not only his Austrian country hoped for an exception from an only-too-often proved rule : the happy survival.

I often think about a vision : of Jochen in later years. A Jochen who *had* escaped to a safe career and a fantastic business life. And Colin Chapman commenting : 'His natural ability would have given him the world title for years and years – but he didn't want it, because he discovered racing to be boring.'

How I wish that vision had become reality.

# CHAPTER FIVE

# Juan Manuel Fangio

## *by* Eric Dymock

*Born in 1934, Eric Dymock describes himself as 'a
student of motor racing' – a course which he has
pursued on both sides of the Atlantic not only for*
The Guardian – *for whom he is motor racing correspondent – but also leading European journals.
Co-author, with Jackie Stewart, of* World Champion.

Fangio ... the name rings through motor racing history. Five
times Champion Driver of the World. Only Jim Clark matched
him in Grand Prix wins. Fangio was the shy champion, who
was 40 when he won his first title, racing difficult cars against
men half his age. Argentinian, bandy-legged, with a thin, high
voice, Fangio was the driver everyone called the maestro. His
personal magnetism persists. Twelve years after he quit racing
he still gets the adulation of crowds, the handshakes, and
whatever he does still makes news. Watch when he visits a
motor race. Other drivers get mobbed, but not Fangio. The
crowds part in front of him, clear a way for a living legend of
the track.

I saw Fangio race but twice. Neither time did he win. But
even from the trackside, you could feel the presence of an
extraordinary human being. Face to face, there is no doubt.
His movements are deliberate, slow, almost indolent. He has a
welcome, restrained smile, and he has the most riveting eyes
of almost anyone I ever met. And always the sing-song voice in
the lilting South American Spanish, full of 'eh's', and soft
consonants.

Fangio, to me and countless more, was a schoolboy hero. I
had read about him for years before I ever heard anyone
(outside the schoolboy circle) utter his name. It took a long

time to lose the habit of pronouncing the 'g' hard. It looked like Fang-gio in the motoring papers of the early 'fifties. They did not leave you in much doubt about what sort of driver he was, even though his lack of English kept him more of an enigma to the motor racing writers of the time than he probably deserved. That only added to the magic. Here was some sort of demon driver from the other side of the world, come to Europe with a genius for handling racing cars that was in the best traditions of schoolboy fiction – a sort of motor racing Cannonball Kydd, with talent for snatching victory by some unbelievable alchemy at the goalmouth. Fangio's dexterity was in the 'Hotspur' class.

Or so it seemed at the time.

The facts are hardly less dramatic.

Juan Manuel Fangio was born on June 24th, 1911 in Balcarce, a small town about 220 miles from Buenos Aires, the fourth of six children in an immigrant Italian family. His father, a house-painter, had left the Abruzzi province of Chieti in Italy when he was only seven. The young Fangio had a passion for engines, which were still something of a novelty in South America during the 'twenties and early 'thirties when he was growing up. He began work as a garage mechanic, surviving severe pneumonia when he was seventeen, until at the age of twenty-one he was called up for military service, and became the CO's driver. What officer ever had such a chauffeur? His pastimes were football and boxing, but already the seeds had been sown of an absorbing enthusiasm for motor racing. A customer of the garage had taken him on a road race as a mechanic. Fangio who was to be five times Champion of the World, took part in his first hot, dusty motor race as a make-weight in the passenger seat of a 1928 Chevrolet.

Following his National Service, Fangio opened a small garage in Balcarce, and in 1934 began driving in road races, Andes versions of the Mille Miglia, but longer, in stages – often taking several days. He drove Ford and Chevrolet V-8 coupes, doing well enough for the villagers in Balcarce to take notice. Whispered congratulations for a good drive, a touch on the arm or a nod for ill-luck.

Juan's parents disapproved. Their son was surely out of his depth in danger.

Yet Balcarce saw in Juan something special. They felt, as many other towns perhaps in a sense of communal pride must have felt, that they had talent in their midst, and in the absence of any rich benefactor who might put up money for the boy's racing, they had a whip-round on their own. 'Peasants,' to use Fangio's own words, 'who would slice a loaf thin to save a penny subscribed enthusiastically.' He said that every time he won a race after that, he felt he had repaid another instalment of his moral debt to Balcarce.

The villagers' talent-spotting was right, they were lucky – they had Fangio. But time was running out. Fangio's imagination had been fired. He knew that Europe was the centre of motor racing and if he was ever even going to see a Grand Prix, that was where he must go. But it was 1939. By 1942 racing, even in South America, had come to a halt. Frustrated, Fangio drove his old Ford furiously over the routes of the pre-war races in the mountains. He was keeping his hand in, afraid only as the years rolled past, that by the time racing resumed, he would be too old.

It was February, 1947, after a lapse of nearly five years before it started again with the Grand Prix of Buenos Aires. Fangio, back in his faithful Chevrolet was third. All through that year he campaigned the old car, preparing it himself, now winning frequently, becoming a local hero, and gaining recognition from the Automobile Club of Argentina.

For the 1948 Argentine Grand Prix races, they bought two Maseratis, one for Oscar Galvez, and the other for Fangio. They raced the cars in Europe but without success. Yet it was clear that the by now 37-year-old Fangio had great promise. His skill had been noticed by his European adversaries, like Villoresi, Varzi, and the great Jean-Pierre Wimille, who observed : 'If one day he has a car that is right for his temperament, Fangio will perform miracles.'

In 1949, it was Europe again with the Maserati, for a more determined assault on the bastions of motor racing. Following a win in the Mar del Plata Grand Prix, Fangio scored a sensational series of victories at San Remo, Pau, Perpignan, Marseilles, Monza, and Albi. He either won or retired. Rivals began to look on him as almost supernatural. He was the general who never lost a battle, the detective who always got his man, the centre-forward whose magic boots never missed a shot. The schoolboy fiction legend had begun.

In 1950 Fangio joined the Alfa Romeo team to drive the Type 159 – one of the best drivers in the world in one of the most successful racing cars of all time. It looked like an invincible combination, and it very nearly was. The first official World Drivers' Championship eluded Fangio narrowly. Instead, it went to Giuseppe Farina in the last race, the Italian Grand Prix at Monza. Fangio had been leading on points, but first his own, and then Taruffi's car let him down.

Fangio's first Championship came in 1951, once again driving for Alfa Romeo, but this time with a formidable 31 points, to Alberto Ascari's 25.

Yet the next year, Alfa withdrew in the face of opposition from Ferrari, and Fangio was out of a job. He had a few races with a Ferrari in South America, and had the usual string of victories, followed by an unsatisfactory drive with BRM. But it was to be an ill-starred year, culminating in his only injury in a racing car. Fangio broke his neck. He had exhausted himself travelling, taken the wheel of a Maserati at Monza, and crashed on the Seraglio.

At first, his comeback was slow. It was late the following May, 1953 before he scored a win at Albi in the BRM. But by the end of the year he was back on form, winning again, it seemed as he pleased. It looked at though it could go on for ever. He won the famous Carrera Panamericana, the Mexican road race so like the long, flat-out blinds on which he had cut his racing teeth years before. He was getting ready for his second Championship, in 1954.

This was the first of his two Mercedes years. Fangio won the Argentine and Belgian Grands Prix for Maserati. Then, when the Silver Arrows swept everything in front of them for the rest of the season, Fangio was there, leading them past the chequered flag in France, Germany, Switzerland, and Italy. He was also second at Berlin, third in Spain, and fourth in the famous race with the streamliner at Silverstone, where he kept knocking the marker cans at the edge of the track.

By now Fangio had been racing over twenty years. He carried on for another four, but two events – the deaths of Felice Bonetto in the 1953 Carrera Panamericana, and then his young

protégé and fellow Argentinian Onofre Marimon during practice for the German Grand Prix in 1954 – reshaped Juan's
thinking.

Drivers tend to accept friends' deaths as inevitable tragedies
– for a time. They are shocked by death on the race track, but
then they lock the event away in their mind, sometimes even
talk about a driver as though he were going to be alongside
them on the grid at the next race. They refer to so-and-so's
'accident', not so-and-so's death.

But there comes a time when their cup is full. There is no
capacity for any more ghosts. Death has come too close. This is
the stage I believe Fangio reached in 1954. Yet his dedication
was such, his professionalism so wholehearted, he had spent
so long reaching his goal that he carried on racing, reaching
new heights of brilliance at the wheel.

In 1955 he retired in only two races – Le Mans, and the
Monaco Grand Prix. In all the other twelve he was either
first or second, and he was only second four times. He only
gave away one Grand Prix, and that was to Stirling Moss at
Aintree on the last corner of the last lap. It was one of these
rare seasons in motor racing where the undisputedly fastest
driver was at the wheel of the undisputedly fastest and most
reliable car.

With three Championships behind him and the withdrawal
of Mercedes-Benz, Fangio went to Ferrari. He won another
Championship but fell out with Enzo Ferrari and so, in 1957,
switched to Maserati. It made no difference; he won the
Championship again, winning ten major races, including the
Grands Prix of Argentina, Buenos Aires, Monaco, Portugal,
France, and Germany, a race that was hailed as the greatest
he ever drove.

But Fangio had only another half dozen or so races left.
After that great victory in Germany, he raced only twice
more in Europe, the Italian Grand Prix, where he came second,
and then in 1958, the French Grand Prix, where Mike
Hawthorn winning in a Ferrari could not bring himself to lap
him in an ailing Maserati just before the finish. Fangio had
never been lapped by anyone in a European Grand Prix.

There seemed to be nothing left for Juan Fangio to do as a
racing driver except perhaps die as a racing driver. It would

be absurd to suggest that he did not realise the risks of going on, and twenty-four years is a long time to avoid the pitfalls, the blow-outs, and mechanical failures, to say nothing of all the other drivers. Yet that is probably not why he retired – not by his understanding anyway. He had accomplished more than any other man in motor racing, and more than any man was likely to accomplish for a long time. Even Clark's record of 25 Grand Prix wins is not strictly comparable because they were done in an era when there were more Grand Prix races. Fangio probably gave it up in a mixture of despair at the deaths of so many fine drivers, and the realisation that he had reached the summit. He was a mountaineer at the conquest of Everest.

In 1958 the names of Collins, Castellotti, and Musso were added to the toll, and whatever else Fangio may have thought, his cup of melancholy overflowed. Most of his grief was still locked away. He reasoned that he was retiring because he was at the top of the tree; motor racing had no mystery left. He had done it all.

Which he had.

It was not a consistently well-planned pursuit of glory. One of the earliest races Fangio drove in showed what a casual affair South American racing was, and also the young village-hero's scant regard for the rules. It was in 1936, and Fangio entered his Model A Ford. But he had had trouble with the ignition and stayed up all night putting it right. He arrived at the start in time for officials to tell him the race had begun. The seven friends he had brought were bundled out of the car, and with a fine disregard for formalities, Juan dashed on to the track, and set the Ford off in pursuit. He was disqualified.

How do you recognise a Champion driver? By lap times and results of course, but that may only tell you if a driver is Champion *class*. The rest you find by talking to him, testing for ambition, dedication, and the extra urge that will make him a race winner, not just a fast driver. Finding a Fangio is something else.

Marcello Giambertone was an Italian journalist watching the cars go through the Parabolica corner at Monza. He was a track marshal during the Grand Prix of the Autodrome in the hot June of 1949, and Fangio had talked to him about the condition of the track at that corner. He knew Fangio was good; knew he was something out of the ordinary because here he was at thirty-eight bursting upon the European scene when most drivers are thinking about giving it up. Ascari had spoken well of Fangio after seeing him race in Argentina.

Giambertone watched the race, together with another official Mario Sorrentino. They realised that Fangio took the corner on exactly the same line, lap after lap with a regularity and precision like no one else.

Giambertone waited for a gap in the traffic, and stuck a match in a crack close to where Fangio's wheels had passed. Lap after lap, Fangio's Ferrari passed within a tyre's width. Lap after lap the variation was insignificant, while other drivers would be feet away.

An instant Fangio fan, Giambertone later became his manager and a close friend.

Did Fangio allow Moss to win the British Grand Prix of 1955? It was a hot day at Aintree, and the Silver Arrows were quite unchallenged. Was there some collusion to let the young British driver win the British Grand Prix, the first ever victory by a home driver? Mercedes-Benz raced for publicity and without doubt the race was highlighted by Moss's win. Fangio had no need of Championship points – he had more than enough. Yet it certainly looked as though the old fox was cunningly out-manoeuvred by the young apprentice as they raced through Melling Crossing.

Fangio could certainly be magnanimous. In his first Alfa Romeo year, 1950 he was entered in the Grand Prix of Pescara, the Coppa Acerbo. There were two Type 159 Alfas, Fangio's and another for Luigi Fagioli, a grizzled but rather luckless veteran, especially that year, and who dearly wanted to win a big race before he retired.

The Alfas had things pretty much their own way. They were doing 193 mph down the straight, and were well ahead, with Fagioli in front. But on the last lap Fagioli's car broke a front spring. They were so far in the lead that Fangio was able to stop. His team-mate's wheel was lying over at an angle, the suspension collapsed. Yet it might *just* reach the finish line.

'Go on,' shouted Fangio. He remained behind the stricken Alfa, grinding along in first gear. Down the Cappelle Pass they came, on to the Monte Silvano Straight, until the buckled wheel finally seized, with only a few hundred yards to go.

Fagioli caught sight of Rosier's Talbot finally making up on them, as he inched his way to the climax of his sporting career. Only when hope was gone did Fangio overtake to ensure an Alfa win.

Abducted at gunpoint in Cuba by Castro supporters to draw world attention to the revolutionaries soon to take the island over, Fangio earned the dubious distinction of being a pioneer political kidnapee. Some of his successors were less fortunate. He was well-treated and released after the Grand Prix was over. He even watched the race on television.

Normally easy-going, one suspects that Fangio's famous quarrel with Enzo Ferrari was more between the huffy, elderly car-builder and Fangio's manager, than with Fangio himself. Yet Ferrari pulls no punches when talking about the Argentinian. He is unflattering about Fangio's voice, describing it as 'tinny', and 'metallic', and recalls meeting him in 1949 when he let Argentine Automobile Club officials do all the talking, meanwhile 'maintaining an inscrutable expression ... and an indefinable squinting smile'. Hardly a promising opinion of a driver who was going to win the 1956 World Championship for Maranello, but perhaps rob it the following year in retribution.

Ferrari says Fangio remained a mystery to him because of his silences, but praised his driving unreservedly. The disagreement arose over Fangio's place in the Ferrari team. Giambertone thought his cars were sometimes less well prepared than Peter Collins's because of the important British market for Ferrari cars. He even suspected sabotage in the Mille Miglia when Fangio's cockpit was flooded. Ferrari's reply was that the holes in the body, cut for brake cooling, did not prevent Castelotti from winning. In the Belgian Grand Prix there were suspicions that Fangio's broken final drive was due to deliberate shortage of oil. Ferrari points out, very fairly, that without oil he could never have led round the enormously fast Spa-Francorchamps track for 21 laps before the failure took place.

Ferrari complains that Fangio had a persecution mania. And he was not the only person Fangio described as devious.

The Italian driver Luigi Villoresi for example, was once accused of baulking Fangio to help Alberto Ascari. Alfa Romeo mechanics were said not to have filled up his fuel tank once, so that Farina might win.

Giambertone insisted that Fangio should have his own mechanic to supervise the work on his car, which cannot have done much to foster good relations between Enzo and Juan. At the end of the World Championship year of 1956, when the firm had won 50 Million Lire from the Italian Automobile Club for the best performance by an Italian constructor, Ferrari had a gold medal struck for each of his drivers – except Fangio. Giambertone's requests for one met with disdain. So perhaps there were faults on both sides.

No such rancour seems to have affected Fangio's relationship with Mercedes-Benz. He continued to import their cars into Argentina, and long maintained connections with Mercedes even after he retired. He often worked for them in a public relations capacity in Europe and South America, Stuttgart being astute enough to keep reminding people of their association with Fangio. They still got a return on the money they spent in motor racing many years after their last race.

Fangio's place in motor racing history is secure. It was not so much his accumulation of wins, but the way he stamped the quality of the whole era. Undoubtedly he made a lot of money from driving, and laid the foundations of a successful and profitable business empire in Argentina. But in some ways he was amongst the last of the 'shirt sleeve' drivers to whom, perhaps mistakenly, safety was not of first importance. He has since admitted to more regard for safety in motor racing, and in an interview for the BBC2 programme *Wheelbase* in 1970, mentioned narrow roads and wide tyres as two hazards which ought to be examined. He said everything had changed completely, and things become much more competitive. Safety lay with the constructors and the FIA, which needed to find ways of making things safer without losing the atmosphere of the race track. Fangio said he felt cars of his day were safer to have accidents in, and he would not have preferred to race in any time but his own.

Yet Fangio remained motor racing's Stanley Matthews until retiring at the age of 47. Retirement was, 'A matter for a driver's conscience ... eventually he must leave his place for others ... must not continue to race, and that is very difficult, quite, quite difficult.'

Aloof, elusive, remote, people have tried to find reasons for Fangio's mastery of the racing car. It has been suggested his coolness is explicable by an abnormally slow heartbeat (it nearly stopped altogether in 1970 when Fangio had a mild heart attack) and by exceptional visual acuity. Jackie Stewart showed a similar emotional control to that claimed for Fangio. A capacity for race-long concentration was another reason given for his superiority, and an ability to grasp everything about a race, the positions of the other cars, his speed, the condition of his engine, and the strategic situation. Fast reactions, even, 'a cat-like anticipation and judgment', stamina, and courage – whatever they were, Fangio had them. He almost certainly ranks above even Nuvolari and Clark, although one must be cautious about comparing drivers of different eras, just as with athletes of different eras, because performance in absolute terms develops with each fresh generation. Take, for example, the four minute mile, once an Olympic barrier, now beaten regularly at national championship level. Motor racing is the same. Nuvolari at his best would probably not have beaten Fangio at *his* best, even in comparable cars. If Fangio had stayed on, he would probably not have been able to match the mature Stirling Moss, who might in turn have been no match for Jim Clark at the same stage of *his* career.

Yet on the evidence of the margins by which Fangio could beat his rivals, it is safe to argue that his standards would not be matched for a long time, perhaps for decades. It is as though Roger Bannister broke four minutes with a mile in 3 minutes 34 seconds, instead of 3 minutes 59 something.

Take that great race at the Nürburgring in 1957, the year of his last Championship, the year before he retired. On August 4th, 1957 there were three young tigers in V-8 Ferraris, the cars now shorn of their Lancia side tanks. They were Peter Collins, Luigi Musso, and Mike Hawthorn. They could go the full distance without refuelling or changing tyres, whereas Fangio's 250F Maserati could not. During practice, Fangio went faster than the old lap record speed; his suspect tyres probably had better grip, their problem was lasting the distance. Twenty-two laps, 310 miles to go, 23 cars on the grid. From lap 3, Fangio was ahead trying to build up a lead on the Ferraris, to anticipate the inevitable pit stop. By half distance he had 28 seconds in hand, then he stopped. Refuelling and a tyre change cost him well over 50 seconds. Collins and Hawthorn forged ahead.

Giambertone takes credit for putting the idea into his head. He suggested that Fangio take it easy for two laps, to suggest trouble. Then, on a signal, he speeded up out of sight of the pits. The Ferrari team manager, Tavoni took the bait, fell for the anxious looks in Fangio's pit, and the halting progress of the Champion. He signalled his cars to keep a steady speed.

The Nürburgring is 14.2 miles round, and the lap times in 1957 were between nine and ten minutes. Once a driver gets an order from the pits, there is no way of countermanding it for another ten minutes of racing.

Choosing his moment, Fangio suddenly speeded up. He turned in a record lap starting from just past the pits, which gave him one lap before he was timed, and another lap before the Ferraris could possibly get a signal saying so. Twenty-eight miles to creep up on them unawares. Tavoni caught on too late. He hung out the FASTER signal to his two young English drivers, but Fangio was out to break records. He broke the 90 mph barrier for the Nürburgring with a lap in 9 minutes 25.3 seconds, beating his best practice time which itself shattered his own 1956 record of 9 minutes 41.6 seconds. Fangio clawed back the Ferrari's lead. On lap 17 he was 25½ seconds behind; on lap 18, 20 seconds; lap 19, 13½ seconds; lap 20 an incredible 3 seconds. The Ferrari pit was frantic. The 'old man' sliced an unprecedented 24.2 seconds off the old record with a time of 9 minutes 17.4 seconds.

He passed Collins coming out of the South Curve, was re-passed, but overtook again almost immediately. Hawthorn fought him off at first, remembering perhaps the epic French Grand Prix at Rheims where he had snatched a hairsbreadth victory from Fangio after a wheel to wheel duel for most of the race. But this was Fangio's day. He never had to repeat his astonishing 9 minutes 17.4 seconds; he had already broken the record ten times that day.

There are more stories about Fangio. His drive in the Mille Miglia with only one wheel steering, his avoidance of a multi car pile-up at Monaco when, in the blink of an eye, he noticed spectators on a blind corner looking the other way, flashing a warning. The terrible moment at Le Mans in 1955, when Pierre Levegh raised his hand to Fangio just behind, a warning of disaster, moments before Levegh's Mercedes-Benz 300 SLR plunged into the crowd, killing over 80 people.

Fangio came through the whole gamut of motor racing experience. And triumphed.

**VICTORY PRELUDE**

Jochen Rindt testing the revolutionary Lotus 72 that was to give him a monopoly of Grand Prix wins in 1970—before the accident that made him the sport's first posthumous Champion.

**DANGER ROUND THE CORNER**

Shortly after this picture was taken, Jochen Rindt crashed in his Lotus-Ford—an accident blamed on the giant wing. Spanish Grand Prix 1969.

A LEGEND AT WORK

Juan Manuel Fangio leading the French Grand Prix at Rouen, 1957, in his Maserati.

DETERMINATION

Denny Hulme presses grimly on in the 1971 Spanish Grand Prix. He finished fifth in his McLaren Ford.

# CHAPTER SIX

# Denny Hulme

## *by* Elizabeth Hayward

*Elizabeth Hayward studied painting, qualified as an
Art teacher, and taught in Grammar Schools. She
wrote articles and short stories from student days
onwards under her real name, Priscilla Bailey.
When she married David Phipps, she was faced
with a choice: (a) stay at home and see husband
rarely; (b) go along to motor races as passenger
and (c) become a motor racing journalist and add
to the joint account. She chose (c) and has not
regretted it. She writes for* Road & Track, Auto
Racing, *and* Sport Auto, *and is Assistant Editor of
the annual,* Autocourse. *She is the only woman
member of the International Racing Press Association. She has two children, aged twelve and eight.
She has had books published on Jackie Stewart
and on Formula One Racing and worked with Jack
Brabham on his autobiography* When the Flag Falls.

'I wish they could have a race with no spectators at all. In
fact, what I most enjoy is going testing. I just have a thrash
around and do what I want. I shun social things because I am
basically shy. I know I ought to go along to all the functions,
dance around and make speeches and all the rest – but I don't
like that one little bit. I *hate* it. Giving speeches is the worst
thing in the world.'

Denis Clive Hulme is a surprisingly complex and sensitive
person, with a great deal to say if he feels he can trust you, and
absolutely no interest in passing the time of day if he doesn't.
In personal relationships he is extremely cautious, as if afraid
of giving too much of himself away. He is stubborn, plain-

spoken in a reasonably quiet way, and can't stand anything phoney.

The worst knock Denny has ever had to take was the death of Bruce McLaren in June 1970; even the disaster of his own injuries sustained at Indianapolis three weeks before, the terribly painful burns on his arms and feet and hands, became insignificant by comparison. Everyone who knew Bruce felt sadly lost without him, but Denny perhaps most of all. He had leaned heavily on Bruce, on his gentleness, his good humour, his knowledge of cars and racing, and when Bruce was killed, the popular image of the tough, indolent, self-contained New Zealander cracked.

Yet within five weeks of his 'Indy' disaster he went to run at Mosport in the first CanAm race of the season, hardly able to curve his charred fingers round the steering wheel – and came third. Most people thought him foolhardy, but for Denny that way was the *only* way – by driving the McLaren in spite of all the cards stacked against him, he was hitting back at Fate, keeping alive the spirit of the McLaren team, and proving to himself that he could cope.

I accused him of being pig-headed, going to Mosport to drive when he couldn't even hold a knife and fork to cut his food; if he gripped anything the newly-formed skin on his fingers split. He agreed with me.

'It runs in the family,' he replied cheerfully. And so it does. His father is one of the select few who earned the Victoria Cross in the Second World War and stayed alive. He was in Crete, a sergeant with the New Zealand Army, and he went off on his own behind the German lines to do a bit of useful sniping. He was wounded and sent home in 1941.

'I'm very much like my father in many ways,' says Denny, 'Terribly stubborn and dogmatic. My mother is the opposite, placid and quiet. It seems to be a Hulme thing. We call a spade a spade, and if there is any kind of a storm or emotional carry-on, we retire into the background until it is over!'

Denis was born in Nelson, South Island, on June 18th 1936.

'I don't remember much about Nelson itself, but I can remember during the war going to my grandmother's farm – my mother's father's farm – at Motueka. That's a real wild place. They grow almost all the tobacco in New Zealand there. I was only about three or four years old, but there are some things I can remember vividly – the whole farm, the shape of it, the old pear tree I once fell out of and knocked myself unconscious. We used to go and sit amongst the tobacco when they picked it, little kids sitting under those giant leaves. The workers used to have drinks of lime juice, made from fresh limes, during the warm days. They just used to put oatmeal into it.

'I ran away one day, about a quarter of a mile from the house, and went across a swing bridge, the sort you see in African jungles, which spanned a huge river. I lay on my stomach and looked down. There were eels swimming around at the bottom of the river and I watched them for ages. I suppose I was about three and a half.

'I remember they had an old fire engine on the farm which they used to drive the circular saw. I watched my grandfather sawing up wood, and wished I were big enough to help. I came along once with a big strip of bark and slung it up on the bench, but it got all wrapped round the saw. My grandfather was livid; I dashed off and hid under the shed until he calmed down.

'They had big tobacco kilns there too, and a stream; and some sheep. I got knocked down by a sheep – they were big Merinos with great long horns. I was just wandering around and minding my own business when bang! One of them butted me and rolled me down the hill. There was a big waterwheel in the stream, too, where they used to charge the batteries, as there was no mains electricity.

'Before the war Dad was a share milker, working on a farm. He didn't own it, maybe he just owned a herd of cows. Anyway, I nearly got drowned there when I was very small. They had to go across a stream to take the cream to the end of the road, and instead of going across the bridge I decided to walk across the ford. I got swept away. Dad fished me out, and turned me upside down to get all the water out, so I only had a fright. It didn't put me off water. These are only unimportant little details, really. You are probably the first person to know about them.'

I didn't think these details at all unimportant. Far from it. I feel that Denny's rural childhood has more to do with the man he is now than anything that happened later, including his discovery of the delights of the motor car. The Grand Prix driver who shuns the jet-set type of life, who tends to sit away from the rest of the motor racing fraternity on planes and go to sleep, who often stays in hotels that only McLaren Racing patronise; who has no outside business interests and prefers, when he gets home, to take his shoes off, put his feet up and watch colour television; he is the product of a country which was *really* country, where outdoor living is considered normal, and children go barefoot not from poverty but from choice and tradition.

'I like being alone. I like to wander around and discover nature. I never preach about it, but I'd like to go where no other human being has gone – very difficult in this modern world. The best thing I've done in recent years was to make a trip with Greeta up Death Valley in America. We stopped the car in the middle of the desert and there wasn't even a vapour trail in the sky. It must have been exciting in the old days, stomping through the world looking for new places...'

When Denny's father returned from the war, invalided out of the Army, he went on a convalescent trip to Rotorua in North Island. While he was there he looked around a bit and returned to Nelson to collect his wife and children – Denis, then nearly six, and Anita, three. They were to move to North Island, to the area round the Bay of Plenty, which has a beautiful Mediterranean-type climate, and wonderful hill and sea views.

'I remember the epic journey we had as we set off from Nelson to live in the North. We had a Morris 8 four-seater tourer. This was the first car I learnt to drive; I'd already driven tractors on farms. All the family belongings were strapped around it and on it, and most of the roads were only gravel. It took us a long time to make the journey because the car kept running out of water at high altitudes. We had to keep going off and hunting for water to stop the radiator from boiling. We made it eventually, in about a day and a half.'

The Hulme family went to live at a place called Pongakawa, 10 miles from the nearest town of Te Puke and 25 miles from Tauranga, the main town on the Bay of Plenty. Clive Hulme,

Denny's father, was given an ex-service loan and started a trucking business, which was a sensible thing to do in the fast-growing, post-war New Zealand. Many ex-servicemen were given parcels of land which they had to clear, build on, and turn into some kind of profitable concern. Clearing the sites and levelling them was part of the Hulme business, and what was once an area of wild beauty around Tauranga has now been tamed, tidied, and built up to such a degree that it bears little resemblance to the place where Denny grew up. There was very little traffic, shoes were only for special occasions, and one's proudest possession would be some land and a vehicle of some sort. And for a boy, a dog.

'I had a cross between a collie and a husky. He was marvellous with sheep. We boys used to go off to the river with our dogs and wade in, quite a gang of us, Maori kids as well. Sometimes we'd spend all day with no clothes on at all – it was so wild there was no one about, and I don't think our mothers worried much about us. Everyone mixed in, swimming and diving amongst the weeds, chasing eels, and getting logs to float down the river. The greatest fun was when the rivers were in flood. Then we'd get the biggest logs we could find, push them into the main stream, get on them and away we would go, crashing down under bridges and swimming to the shore when we got tired and walking back again.

'I have seen a lot of the world from my small beginnings, and looking back I can see that my childhood did me no harm. In fact it was the sort of childhood a lot of people would love to have had; different. We had to make our own entertainment all the time, whether it were with sledges, or playing around the hills or in the rivers . . . or the drains! We used to go home filthy, but our mothers never really gave us a growling. It was part of life out there, they expected their kids to get dirty. Over here people are so fussy.'

The other big influence in the life of the growing lad was his father's trucking business. He owned two Ford V8 trucks at first, then he bought two ex-Army Chevrolets with Timken 2-speed rear ends. Vehicles of any sort were very scarce in New Zealand during and after the war, and these two were quite a prize. They used to use them for a variety of things – moving sheep, carrying super-phosphates out to the farmers

around, and carting sand to Rotorua are just three examples.
The Rotorua contract was one of the most important. Everything there had to be built of concrete because iron can't stand
up to the sulphur problem from the hot underground springs.
It was a 100 mile round trip from the Hulme homestead,
and the roads were very bad. But journeys like this with
his father taught Denny a lot about driving in difficult
circumstances and a great deal about practical motor
mechanics.

In 1953 Mr Hulme sold the Chevrolets and bought a Morris
truck which had a Swiss diesel engine, a Saurer.

'Of course, they were very rare. Nobody knew much about
diesels. So I got a workshop manual and learned how to maintain the engine. I also learned how to drive, officially, and
passed my test at 15, in a Chrysler. At 17 I was driving heavy
trucks of sheep to the sheep trains every Sunday – illegally.
You can't have a heavy traffic licence until you are 18, but the
local police tended to turn a blind eye. During the week I
went to school, but I wasn't too bright. I didn't learn much.
When I was 17 they were recruiting for the New Zealand Air
Force, and I tried to get in, but I guess they thought I was too
dumb. Anyway I never heard from them after going to the
recruiting office! A few days later Dad dropped a huge concrete cattle trough on his foot and couldn't drive. As the
family lived on the business, Dad said I'd better leave school,
and take over the driving till he was better.'

When he was 18 it was decided that he should work in a
garage that was 'up the road', just Denny and the owner.

'It sounds a small affair, but we got through a tremendous
amount of work, from rebores on cars to repairing bulldozers.
It was terribly expensive to get new parts so we made a lot.
I got quite a good tan, welding. But nobody told me you
shouldn't take off your shirt or walk around barefoot when
you are welding. My skin got so tough I didn't feel the hot
pieces when they flew.

'I worked in the garage all day and shifted sand for Dad
at night. It was hard work. During my lunch break I used to
drive the seven miles up to the beach, shovel six and a half
tons of sand and drive back, eating an apple in the cab on
the way home. That's how I got big shoulders and these thick

arms. They come in quite useful driving in Formula One.'

Cars, as opposed to trucks, hardly existed for Denny until a friend of his, who had some connection with MG's, talked endlessly about this particular make and stirred Denny's interest in getting some transport of his own. By now he had managed to save £450 ($1,080), quite a lot for a youngster, and he set his heart on an MG TF.

One day his father simply said, 'How would you like to go to Auckland and pick up your new car?'

Denny was flabbergasted, but his father explained that three new MG's had arrived at the docks and all his son had to do was ring up the agent and tell him which one he wanted – the white, the red, or the green. The red one had disc wheels and was £28 ($67.25) cheaper, so Denny chose that.

'I hitch-hiked up to Auckland, which was over 130 miles, one Saturday morning to pick it up. It was still covered with grease, just as it had come from England, and was to me the greatest thing in the world. I drove away in it, choosing the longest way back. I'd never seen a car with a rev counter before and it wasn't until I'd done about 40 miles that I realised I'd been looking at that instead of the speedometer. I drove the car about 1,000 miles that week-end, just for the fun of it.'

Denny was to keep that red MG for three years. In the second year he joined the local car club and became interested in competition. He found he could beat all-comers, and, almost in spite of himself, he found himself on the road that led to the World Championship. But initially it was the mechanical side of the MG he was interested in. He loved tinkering with it, bought the BMC workshop manual, and tuned it 'by the book', plus a little on his own initiative, and it was very successful.

His next car was an MGA, but it was less competitive than the TF and Denny decided to trade it in for a 2-litre Cooper-Climax which Bruce McLaren had raced the previous year. He seemed destined to become a racing driver.

'The family never deterred me. In fact they always encouraged me, and used to travel miles to see me race. I bought a Cooper in March, which is the end of the season out there, and I wouldn't be racing it until November. So I proceeded to pull it to pieces, never having seen a Cooper-Climax before! I stripped the whole car and built a special garage for it, a proper brick one with benches, and all the tools nicely lined up. It is Dad's pride and joy even to this day. I did all the work on the car myself, even the engine, which was a hell of a job. But, maybe more by luck than judgment I got it all right, put it together, painted it and went racing.'

He raced so successfully that season, 1959–60, that he was put forward as a candidate for the 'Driver to Europe' scheme, by which the New Zealand International Grand Prix Association had sent Bruce McLaren to England the year before. The other candidate was George Lawton, who was generally accepted as being quicker than Denny, but there was so little in it that both young men came over to England to try their luck.

'In the first three years I was over here I nearly gave up many times. George was killed in practice for the Roskildering race in 1960, and I then teamed up with Angus Hyslop, who was sent from New Zealand under the 1960–61 'Driver to Europe' scheme. We travelled with Formula Junior Coopers all over Europe during the summer and went back home for the Tasman series in the winter.'

1962 was not a good year. Denny's old Cooper was not competitive, and although he was given occasional drives in the Tyrrell Coopers, with modest success, his bread and butter came from his job as a mechanic in Jack Brabham's garage in Chessington. Phil Kerr was Jack's manager there, and the two New Zealanders became good friends. Phil had a lot of faith in Denny's driving ability, and tried to get Jack to give Denny a chance, but it was not until the regular Brabham driver, Gavin Youl, broke his collarbone that Denny got his drive. He took pole position and fourth place in a Formula Junior Brabham at Crystal Palace.

Jack reluctantly agreed that Phil might be right – this raw recruit was able to drive a racing car. He set him up as a one-man outfit with a factory FJ car.

'If Greeta hadn't been here I'd have gone home that year, 1963. She had been at school with me in New Zealand but I met her again when I went home for the 1961–62 Tasman series and then she came over to be a nurse in London. One day late in 1962 we had a serious discussion about what we should do. I'd had to sell my car in order to live and I was very short of money. I wanted to go home but Greeta encouraged me to go on trying. Then I got this car from Jack Brabham and we decided to get married and go racing together.'

They went racing, Greeta acting as time-keeper, pit-signaller, chief-cook-and-bottle-washer, laundry maid and nurse. They came through 1963 with seven wins out of 14 starts. There was new hope of making it to the top rungs of motor racing and all talk of going home was given up.

In 1964 and 1965 Denny drove Formula Two Brabhams with Jack, while Jack and Dan Gurney were the Formula One drivers. At the end of 1965 Dan went off to build his own AAR Eagles and Denny moved up to join Jack in the Formula One team. 1966 was a vintage year for Brabhams. In Formula Two the pair were virtually unbeatable and Jack won his third World Championship. But Denny was sometimes faster than his boss, and this caused a certain amount of bitterness on Denny's part, because he felt he was having 'second car luck'.

In 1967 Denny and Jack raced in the same team but against each other, and Denny won the title. He was first in Monaco and Germany, and picked up enough second and third places to take the Championship. He was consistent, the car was strong, and he was no longer content to be second best.

Being World Champion brought new problems; he was expected to turn into a witty speaker, a party-goer and fête-opener almost overnight. This was agony for Denny Hulme, and still is, though since Bruce's death he has had to be the McLaren team leader and spokesman. He has matured and become less retiring, and his speeches are now precise, pithy, and a joy to hear. But in 1967 things were different.

'I know I didn't cash in on being Champion. I sometimes regret it. I used to listen to other people making speeches and thought, "I could do that," but somehow I feel it doesn't come across when I say anything in public.'

After 1967 began the famous partnership with Bruce McLaren, two New Zealanders who complemented each other to perfection. The orange McLarens dominated the Can Am series for three years on the trot, Bruce taking the title twice and Denny once, both drivers coming first or second at almost every race. Then Bruce was killed testing the 1970 Can Am car, the M8D, at Goodwood in June, while Denny was still nursing his horrific burns, and Denny went doggedly off on the trail with first Gurney and then Peter Gethin as team-mates. He won the title again, and might well be very proud of the fact. But he seldom says much about his driving except to state whether he enjoyed it or not.

Formula One with McLarens has been safe and competitive, and in 1968 Denny almost won the Championship title again, but was put out of the running at Mexico by a collision with a guard rail when a rear damper broke. In 1970 he finished fourth in the Championship table in spite of his burnt hands and in spite of missing two Grands Prix altogether.

He enjoys racing in the States more than in Europe.

'It is something like a club – a bit like New Zealand racing, I suppose. I think the nice thing is that everyone is so relaxed. They get big crowds, the weather is usually very good, and everyone treats the meeting a bit like a festival – the crowd stays on after the racing for a barbecue, or dancing on the track, or something similar. There is a fabulous atmosphere. But I wouldn't want to live over there – I like living in England, I don't know why. It has its drawbacks, but it also has *something*.'

This 'something' has made Denny buy a piece of land in the most expensive part of the South East, St George's Hill near Weybridge, and have his own ultra-modern house built. It is a split-level, plate glass and timber palace, incorporating every gadget and labour-saving device known to science. It has taken him a long time to reap the rewards of motor racing, and after seven years in a flat in Surbiton, he and his family will find it blissfully spacious. Greeta is very proud of her husband's prowess as a handyman and part-time designer/architect who is keeping a beady eye on the final stages of the house-building at the moment. They hope to move in with four-year-old Martin and baby Adele soon.

Has he ever thought of retiring from motor racing? Like all drivers he says he will face that when he feels he is not enjoying racing any more.

'One day I'll give it up. I'll just say, "enough," and that will be it. I shall be off. Where to? I don't know. Probably New Zealand. I certainly don't want to go on to be a millionaire or anything. I am quite happy with what I have. Maybe a little more would be nice . . .

'I think I might like to own a farm, raising beef stock. I never wanted to milk cows!

'I haven't done as well in society, maybe, as I ought to have done. I know the people I really have to know – which is about three – but I don't like small talk and I haven't time for people who just sit down and talk about nothing, putting on as big a front as they can. No way.'

That is one of Denny's favourite expressions. He can be a difficult man when he feels like it – immovable *and* bad tempered. He won't be pushed, or brow-beaten, and if he thinks his life is getting in the least complicated he will retreat into his shell. Racing, testing, visiting the McLaren factory and the building site, plus all the travelling involved in going to race meetings, that is all the complication Denny requires in his life, thank you. He has tremendous stamina, guts and persistence, but he is also very human – kindly, honest, and trustworthy.

'When they asked me to come over to England in 1961 I said, "Who the hell wants to go to England?" I'd never wanted to travel. But I got on the boat and I came. It has been hard work at times, and sometimes I wish I was back home shovelling sand. But I've never *really* regretted it.'

# CHAPTER SEVEN

# Mike Hawthorn

## *by* Philip Turner

*Philip A. Turner went to his first motor race, the Southport 100, in 1931. He began reporting and photographing races in 1936 as Sports Editor of* Motor News, *a Manchester motoring monthly, and has been doing so ever since, save for the war years. He reported the rebirth of motor racing after the war for* Autocar *from 1944–47. He joined* Motor *in 1953 and was appointed Sports Editor at the end of 1959. He has covered heaven only knows how many Grands Prix, well over a hundred.*

When Mike Hawthorn first competed in a Continental Grand Prix, the Ferrari team consisted of Ascari, Farina and Villoresi and the cars without exception all had their engines at the front. It seems a very long time ago, but in fact less than twenty years have gone by. And yet at that time British cars and British drivers just did not count in Grand Prix racing. Mike Hawthorn changed all that, at least in so far as the drivers are concerned. He was the first Englishman since Seaman to be asked to join a top ranking Continental Grand Prix team, the first since Segrave to win a first-class Grand Prix. In spite of these signs of the complete professional, Hawthorn himself always maintained that he was an amateur racing driver, that by profession he was a garage proprietor.

He certainly looked the part of the amateur, happiest when dressed informally, leaning on the counter of some small country pub with a pint of mild-and-bitter in one hand, a pipe clenched between his teeth and his boxer dog at his heel. He was a very big man, 6 ft. 2 in. in height and massively built. When hopping mad, as he sometimes was, he looked very dangerous indeed, but that was not very often. Usually, he stood there, stooping slightly, as tall men do who have contacted so many low roof beams, and probably roaring with laughter at some tale or other, a very relaxed person.

Hawthorn's racing career lasted for eight years, for his first speed event was the Brighton Speed Trials in September, 1950 and his final race was the Moroccan Grand Prix on October 19, 1958, in which he finished second – thereby winning the 1958 World Championship of Drivers. On which high note he retired, only to die in a road accident on January 22nd, 1959.

He was born in Yorkshire, at Mexborough in the West Riding on April 10th, 1929. His father, Leslie who tuned and raced motor cycles, bought the TT Garage at Farnham, Surrey, in 1931 and moved south with his young family. It was in and around the garage that Hawthorn grew up. He went to Ardingly College, Sussex, and while still at school was presented with a 125 cc motor cycle by his father. The 125 was succeeded by a 250 cc Triumph on which Hawthorn transported himself to and from the Dennis commercial vehicle works at Guildford when he began a four year apprenticeship there at the age of 17. From Dennis Brothers he went to Kingston Technical College and then to the College of Aeronautical Engineering at Chelsea from whence so many other budding racing drivers have come.

Hawthorn's first car was a Fiat 500, which in turn gave place to a most decrepit Riley 9 saloon. The Riley engine of that period, with its two high placed camshafts operating the valves through short pushrods, its high performance head design with hemispherical combustion chambers and the inlet and exhaust ports on opposite sides of the head, had an irresistible appeal for motor cyclists, for tuning a single cylinder engine as opposed to a V-12 with four overhead camshafts means there are far fewer variables to play with, but does emphasise the vital part played by each component. Especially the cylinder head. So, when Leslie Hawthorn bought his son first a Riley 9 saloon and then a Riley Imp, he was merely following in the footsteps of other racing motor cyclists who had turned to four wheels, such as, for example, Freddy Dixon.

It was with the 1,100 cc Imp that Mike Hawthorn drove in

his first event, the Brighton Speed Trials of September, 1950. He won his class, even though competing against Harry Lester's much lighter Lester-MG.

By the end of 1950, Stirling Moss and Peter Collins who were both to feature so prominently in Hawthorn's racing career, were already well established. Both were making their mark in the Formula Three of those days which was for 500 cc motor cycle engined single seaters with the engine mounted behind the driver. On reflection, it is perhaps surprising that ace motor cycle tuner Leslie Hawthorn did not launch his son into racing through this motor ex-cycle engined formula. Instead, Mike Hawthorn made his entry into the sport at the wheel of the Riley Imp and the bigger 1½-litre Riley TT Sprite which his father had bought at the same time to drive himself.

Hawthorn therefore learnt the art of race driving at the wheel of pre-war sports cars rather than driving the tremendously competitive 500 cc single-seaters in which driving tactics were much rougher than in sports car racing. Some drivers who have come to Grand Prix racing via sports cars rather than graduating through the current Formula Three single seaters never become really accustomed to racing in very close company with their rivals and often are not very good at getting through race traffic and overtaking, two lessons which the junior league single seater formulae certainly teach drivers. In Hawthorn's case, however, the lack of a Formula Three beginning to his racing had no effect on his driving and in fact he particularly distinguished himself throughout his career by his wheel-to-wheel fights with his rivals. Perhaps the only occasion on which his lack of Formula Three experience showed was when later in his career he competed in a small Lotus sports car at a Brands Hatch meeting and was then horrified by the bumping and boring and other rough tactics employed by his rivals, who were mostly ex-Formula Three drivers.

Although Leslie Hawthorn had intended keeping the 1½-litre Riley for his own use, a strained back kept him out of its cockpit in 1951 and so Mike drove it instead. This was indeed one of those ill-winds, for whereas the 1,100 cc car was barely competitive in its class, the 1½-litre Riley was capable of outright wins, and it is race victories rather than class wins that attract attention to a new driver.

With the 1½-litre Riley, Hawthorn won the 10-lap sports car handicap on the Dundrod circuit, a race held just before the Ulster Trophy for Grand Prix cars, so all the top people were there watching. He also won the Leinster Trophy and competed in the Curragh races. These Irish events were giving him the invaluable experience of driving on real road circuits, whereas so many of his would-be rivals raced only on airfield circuits, which usually provide so much more room for driving errors. Hawthorn also drove regularly in BARC Goodwood meetings where he won the *Motor Sport* Brooklands Memorial Trophy by his consistent performances.

So, by the winter of 1951, the end of Hawthorn's first full season, it was evident that Mike had talent. The next stage was all-important, for somehow, the money had to be found to buy a single-seater for the 1952 season. So many young drivers lose their way at this stage, lack of money keeping them in sports cars or saloons in which they do little more than stagnate. However, it was at this point that Hawthorn had a quite exceptional stroke of luck. A friend of the family was Bob Chase, a Brighton marine engineer who took a considerable interest in motor racing in general and Mike Hawthorn's career in particular.

In bed with a severe cold, Bob Chase took the opportunity to catch up with his reading, and his reading included the motoring magazines which in January, 1952 carried full descriptions of the new 2-litre Cooper-Bristol single-seater designed for the then current Formula Two for unblown 2-litre cars. He at once telephoned the Hawthorns and offered to buy one for Mike to race if the Hawthorns would agree to maintain it.

First meeting for the new car was to be the Goodwood Easter Monday gathering. When its construction fell behind schedule, Mike and his mechanic went to the Cooper works and helped complete it. Similar owner-driver last minute builds are not unknown even today. The Cooper-Bristol was indeed a most suitable car for a novice single seater driver. The power to weight ratio, around 130 bhp propelling 11½ cwt – was sufficient to provide a very lively performance and yet not so excessive as to demand a very delicate throttle foot. The handling, too, was predictable and vice free, and the car could be rushed through corners at a great rate.

Of course, that Easter Monday meeting is now part of motor racing history, for it provided one of the very few examples of a driver achieving instant fame. And that driver was Mike Hawthorn. Before Easter Monday, he was completely unknown to the vast majority of motor racing people, was just a promising club driver to those who kept a sharp eye open for potential talent. By Easter Monday evening he was the most talked about racing driver in Britain. In his first race of the day, the six lap Lavant Cup scratch race for 2-litre cars, Hawthorn went straight into the lead to win from the better known Alan Brown and Eric Brandon who were also driving Cooper-Bristols.

In the six lap Formula Libre race for the Chichester Cup, the opposition was more formidable and included such well-known British drivers of the time as A. P. R. Rolt, Philip Fotheringham-Parker and Denis Poore with a 3.8-litre Alfa. Once again, Hawthorn went out in front and stayed there. The main race of the day was the 12 lap Richmond Trophy for the then current Formula One cars, ($1\frac{1}{2}$-litres supercharged or $4\frac{1}{2}$-litres unsupercharged). This time, it was the burly Argentinian driver, Froilan Gonzales, who shot into the lead and held it at the wheel of Tony Vandervell's special $4\frac{1}{2}$-litre Ferrari, the Thinwall Special. But it was Mike Hawthorn who pursued him throughout in second place – where his 2-litre Cooper-Bristol had no business to be – in front of all the other Formula One cars.

Although Hawthorn was to win other British races with the Cooper-Bristol that season, it was his fourth place in his first Continental race, the Belgian Grand Prix, that was to have more effect on his future. That he was able to go Grand Prix racing with a Formula Two car was the outcome of the very odd state of Grand Prix racing in 1952. In theory, the $1\frac{1}{2}$-litre supercharged and $4\frac{1}{2}$-litre unsupercharged formula still had two years to run, but the withdrawal of the $1\frac{1}{2}$-litre Alfa-Romeo 159 team at the end of the 1951 season left the works $4\frac{1}{2}$-litre Ferraris with no rivals to race against – with the possible exception of the $1\frac{1}{2}$-litre BRM V-16. When, however, the

PRESSING ON

Mike Hawthorn, Ferrari, battling to beat his friend and rival Peter Collins in the 1958 British Grand Prix at Silverstone. On this occasion Mike had to be content with second place.

CONQUEROR OF SPA

Jim Clark en route to another of his 'traditional' wins at Spa—home of the Belgian Grand Prix in 1967. He won there no fewer than FOUR times.

### THE END OF AN ERA

GIANT wings may have been all right for an experienced pilot like Jack Brabham—but they were banned after the 1969 Spanish Grand Prix.

### A CLOSE RUN THING

Two of the greatest exponents ever to come from 'Down Under'. Jack Brabham (right) keeps a close watch on his former protégé Denny Hulme in the 1969 Spanish Grand Prix.

BRM had been unable to get to the starting line of the Italian Grand Prix the previous September, the race organizers with one accord had decided the only safe course was to run the Championship Grands Prix for Formula Two cars in 1952.

Dominating the 1952 Grand Prix scene were the Ferrari team of Ascari, Farina, Villoresi and Taruffi driving the four cylinder 2-litre Ferrari which developed around 230 bhp at 7,000 rpm. So great was this domination that the Grands Prix were in effect two races in one, the outright victory by Ferrari and then the race for the highest placed non-Ferrari.

Driving on the very difficult Spa-Francorchamps circuit in pouring rain, Hawthorn's fourth place was thus much more meritorious than it sounds, for he was beaten by only one non-Ferrari, Manzon's Gordini, and finished ahead of all the other British drivers. Moreover, this drive brought Mike to the attention of the Ferrari team, as he found out when by chance he stayed at the same hotel as the Ferrari people for the Dutch Grand Prix, for it was there that they made the first overtures to him. These overtures by September developed into a firm invitation to try a Ferrari at the Modena circuit. This he did, found it delightful, then made the great mistake of driving round the circuit in his Cooper-Bristol and driving it like a Ferrari. A brake locked going into a corner – the brakes with the drums integral with the wheels were always a weak point on the earlier Cooper-Bristols – and the car went sideways into the straw bales and threw Hawthorn out on to the road. He escaped from this his first major accident with numerous grazes, though he later developed fluid in one lung which kept him in hospital for a time.

In spite of this contretemps, Ferrari were still eager for him to drive for the team but Hawthorn hesitated. Most drivers would have been quite overcome by the honour of being asked to join the Ferrari team, but Hawthorn still hoped there might be a competitive British car for him to drive in Grands Prix. Only when it became obvious there would not be, did he finally sign for Ferrari.

Just as he had made racing headlines in his first single-seater season by his victories at the Goodwood Easter Monday meeting, so again in 1953 with one single victory Hawthorn made the front page of newspapers all over the world when he won the French Grand Prix in his first year in the Ferrari team. For a British driver to win a Continental Grand Prix was enough to surprise the world – to win after a wheel-to-wheel duel with Juan Manuel Fangio after leaving Gonzales Ascari and Villoresi in his wake bordered on the miraculous.

Looking at the race from this distance in time, however, it must be admitted that fast circuits such as Rheims flatter the young driver with a heavy right foot, swift reactions and the outstanding daring of the relatively inexperienced – older drivers often shudder at the risks they took early in their careers. At Rheims Hawthorn diced wheel-to-wheel with Fangio and won, but in the German Grand Prix at the Nürburgring a few weeks later, when they again raced together for lap after lap, Fangio eventually went ahead and Hawthorn just could not hold him on what Mike described as the toughest all-round test of car and driver among the regular racing circuits.

Incidentally, although Hawthorn is these days usually regarded as the epitome of the dashing young driver, far removed from the safety conscious GPDA Grand Prix driver of today, in fact he was probably more concerned about safety in motor racing than any of his contemporaries. He severely criticised the protection for spectators at the Ring, even though he liked driving there.

Altogether, 1953 was a very successful season for a young driver in his first year in the crack Ferrari team, with third places in the German and Swiss Grands Prix, fourth places in the Dutch and Italian Grands Prix and fifth in the British Grand Prix at Silverstone after the most monumental spin nearly the whole length of the pit straight after losing the car coming out of Woodcote.

As a Ferrari team member, Hawthorn also had to drive in sports car races, a branch of motor racing which never greatly appealed to him in spite of the fact that some of his greatest drives were in sports cars. In this, his first Ferrari season, for instance, he shared the wheel of the winning car in both the Belgian 24 Hours and the Pescara 12 Hours.

At the end of 1953, Mike Hawthorn was on the crest of the wave. He had thoroughly justified his inclusion in the Ferrari team, he had won his first Grand Prix and been awarded the British Racing Drivers' Club Gold Star as the most successful British driver. All seemed set fair for the future. Alas, 1953 was the last truly happy year of Hawthorn's life for many a long day.

For 1954 was a year black with disaster. Hawthorn was attacked in Parliament by name at the beginning of the year for dodging his military call-up. He was attacked by the mean-minded and spiteful and defended by the totally in-competent among the politicians when all the time the full facts were available to show that he had already been turned down on medical grounds owing to a kidney complaint for which he was later operated on in hospital.

Then in the Syracuse Grand Prix in April he slammed into the straw bales, the filler cap of the fuel tank sprang open and fuel splashed into the cockpit and exploded in flame. Hawthorn leapt from the blazing car in flames and rolled over and over on the ground to extinguish them. He sustained second degree burns on both legs and his left hand, wrist and elbow. From the professional racing driver's point of view, burns are about the worst injury he can suffer. Not only are they intensely painful, they also take far, far longer to heal properly than seems possible. With the result that most drivers return to the wheel with their burns not yet fully healed and suffer renewed agonies in every race they drive for the rest of the season.

Hawthorn was out of action until June, then just as he was about to return to racing, his father, who had played so great a part in his early racing career, was killed in a road accident on the way home from the Goodwood Whit Monday meeting. It was a terrible homecoming for Hawthorn, still only partly healed from his burns and with the row over his call-up still rumbling on.

Moreover, the family garage business was now Hawthorn's entire responsibility – though his mother agreed to look after it with the help of a manager while Mike continued to race. From now on, however, he had this additional worry, for he was most anxious that the business should continue to thrive so that it would be able to support him when he retired from racing.

Hawthorn rejoined the Ferrari team for the Belgian Grand

Prix at Spa and secured one of his many second places that season in spite of being overcome by fumes from a damaged exhaust system. This was the year Mercedes returned to Grand Prix racing, and for the most part the Italian Ferrari and Maserati teams were outclassed. Hawthorn did achieve one Ferrari victory – in the Spanish Grand Prix at the end of the season.

For the new 2½-litre formula which came into operation at the start of the 1954 season, Ferrari relied at first on enlarged versions of the four cylinder Formula Two cars of the previous year, but with their 2½-litre engines now developing 235 bhp at 7,000 rpm. A completely new car had been developed for the new formula, however, with the fuel carried in side tanks between the wheels instead of in the tail which gave it a rounded, whale like shape, hence its nickname of the Super Squalo. Unfortunately, this concentration of weight between the wheels made it a brute to drive, it being very twitchy, and the drivers all hated it. It is odd that both the latest Ferrari and the new Lancia Grand Prix car which made its appearance towards the end of the season should be notable for their compactness achieved by a short wheelbase and side-mounted fuel tanks. And both the Lampredi designed Ferrari and the Jano-designed Lancia, with their low polar moment of inertia, were difficult to drive, going round fast corners in a series of twitches. Hawthorn was fortunate in that he began his Grand Prix career on relatively low-powered cars which had pleasant handling characteristics.

If 1954 had been a year of personal disasters for Hawthorn, 1955 was a season full of racing disasters for him. When Vanwall offered him a contract to drive their Grand Prix car and Jaguar a contract for sports car racing for 1955, he decided to accept and leave Ferrari, for driving for two English teams meant that he could spend more time in England and therefore take a more active part in running his garage business. Unhappily, the Vanwall was not yet raceworthy, and after some disastrous experiences, Hawthorn had a row with Tony Vandervell and left the team after the Belgian Grand Prix. Ferrari took him back into the fold, but this was a season of complete Mercedes domination and the Super Squalo was in constant trouble.

Hawthorn continued to drive Jaguar sports cars, and it was at the wheel of a Jaguar D that he drove his best races of the year. His tremendous duel with Fangio's Mercedes in the opening hours of Le Mans that year was one of the greatest drives of Hawthorn's career, but it has, of course, been entirely overshadowed by the terrible disaster in which it culminated when Hawthorn came into his pit to refuel after building up a substantial lead over Fangio. Macklin swerved to avoid Hawthorn's Jaguar as it braked for its pit and the Austin-Healey was struck by Levegh's Mercedes approaching at high speed from behind. The Mercedes was launched into the air by the glancing blow, struck the bank opposite the pits and disintegrated, its front axle and suspension scything through a packed public enclosure. To a person as sensitive as Hawthorn, the terrible scene was almost beyond bearing. Although the full inquiry held later completely exonerated him from blame, Hawthorn stumbled from the cockpit into his pit with tears streaming down his face, swearing he would never drive again. That great and steadfast character F. R. 'Lofty' England, who was then Jaguar's team manager, remained completely calm and in control and thus managed to soothe Hawthorn and to convince him that he must take the wheel again if he was to retain his nerve. When co-driver Ivor Bueb brought the Jaguar in at the end of his spell, Hawthorn took over again, and the pair went on to win. There were no victory celebrations, and an awful silence settled over the circuit when the race ended. Hawthorn escaped from everyone to the little bar in the press stand where, surrounded by a little group of his friends among the British journalists, we talked about the opening battle of the race which was still so vivid to him ... of how he had twice lost the Jaguar in long high speed slides during his battle with Fangio, and of how, to his surprise, he found the Jaguar would draw away from the Mercedes down the straights. Hawthorn was by then quite sure in his own mind that he had acted correctly during those vital seconds when he braked for his pit, and that though disaster had then followed, this was the result of a set of tragic circumstances that arose from the running of cars of widely differing performance at Le Mans and from the narrowness of the road past the pits.

Towards the end of the season, Hawthorn drove another

tremendous race with the Jaguar D when he and Desmond Titterington took on the entire Mercedes team with a single Jaguar entry in the Tourist Trophy on the Dundrod circuit in Northern Ireland. The Jaguar led the Mercedes team for many laps and was holding a secure second place when the crankshaft broke on the penultimate lap after the engine had deliberately been run at 6,000 rpm instead of the normal 5,800. Even then, all was well until a gear slipped out of engagement and the revs soared to 6,400 rpm which was just too much.

Hawthorn thought the Jaguar was far superior to any contemporary Ferrari sports car and therefore wanted to continue driving Jaguars in sports car races in 1956. Ferrari would not agree to this, so once again Hawthorn left the Ferrari Grand Prix team and joined BRM. The four cylinder 2½-litre BRM at this time was probably the fastest Grand Prix car. It was also very prone to breaking its outsize valves, and when the engine was running properly then either the universal joints in the rear drive shafts or the single rear disc brake on the transmission were liable to fail. Not surprisingly, Hawthorn had a thoroughly bad Grand Prix season in which he was lucky to escape with his life on several occasions when the BRM suffered one or other of its failures.

He rejoined Ferrari for 1957, his team mates being Peter Collins and Luigi Musso. The Ferrari team cars were now based on the Jano-designed Lancias which were handed over to Ferrari in 1955 when financial difficulties forced Lancia to quit racing. They were brutes to drive, understeering so violently into a corner that the driver had to lift off, but as soon as he did so they oversteered equally violently. Moreover, by now the V-8 engines were down on power by comparison with the Vanwalls and the latest 250F Maseratis. Not surprisingly, therefore, Hawthorn scored a number of second and third places, but no wins.

For 1958, however, Ferrari produced a new Grand Prix car, the Dino V-6, which was based on the successful 1½-litre Dino V-6 Formula Two car. At the start of the season, the new car seemed very promising, being very much easier to drive than the Lancia based V-8s and with plenty of power. But as sometimes happens with a racing car, subsequent development 'disimproved' the cars, introducing violent understeer into the handling and a trying vibration period in the engines at around 7,200 rpm. Hawthorn sat himself down and wrote angry letters of complaint to Enzo Ferrari.

Much work was then done on the cars and by the Belgian Grand Prix they were competitive again, and in the French Grand Prix Hawthorn won his first Grand Prix for some time. It was not a happy victory, however, for his team mate Musso went off the track at high speed and died on the way to hospital. Although the French Grand Prix was to be Hawthorn's only Grand Prix victory of the season, he was finishing in second place so consistently to the Vanwalls that he was running neck and neck with Moss for the World Championship. In the German Grand Prix, however, Hawthorn suffered another grievous personal tragedy when his great friend, Peter Collins, crashed just in front of him and sustained injuries from which he died later in hospital.

Although still deeply distressed by the death of Collins, Hawthorn finished second in the next Grand Prix in Portugal in spite of brake failure, and was again second in the Italian Grand Prix in spite of damaging the clutch at the start. Hawthorn had hoped to win this race and clinch the Championship, but he was never very good at racing starts and over-anxiety on this occasion, heightened when the 30 seconds to go signal was given twice, meant that he began the race with a clutch that had been slipped too much. So that left the final race of the season, the Grand Prix of Morocco, in which Hawthorn had only to finish second to Moss to win the Championship. Moss drove a magnificent race to win and set the fastest lap, thereby giving Vanwall the Formula One Constructors' Championship, but Hawthorn aided by his team-mate Phil Hill finished second and so won the Championship.

When Hawthorn came into his pit and told the Ferrari team chief that this was his last race as he had decided to retire, Tavoni did not believe him. But Hawthorn was in earnest. In appearance, Mike Hawthorn was the happy extrovert, with his massive build, his fair hair and readiness for devilment at post-race parties. But those who knew Hawthorn better realised that behind this façade was a very sensitive person indeed. He was therefore deeply affected by the death of his friends in motor racing – and the deaths had been so many. Of his fellow Ferrari drivers, Ascari, Portago, Castelotti, Musso and Collins had all been killed. Of his English friends, Julien Crossley and his immediate protégè, Don Beauman had died in racing accidents. The death of his great friend Collins was the final straw and he had had enough. He had reached the limit of sorrow.

Not that Hawthorn intended to turn his back on motor racing, for he hoped to take a hand in the organisational side of the sport. He had a great and real feeling for fine cars. Two of his most prized possessions were a 1931 2.3-litre Le Mans Alfa and the 1½-litre Riley Sprite with which he had begun his racing career. He had carefully stripped and rebuilt both cars during his scanty leisure time at his garage, and today both are preserved in the Montagu museum at Beaulieu as the finest possible memorial to a great driver.

How does Hawthorn rate as a driver, not only among his contemporaries but also among the all time 'greats'? In the seven years in which he was competing in Grands Prix he won only three – the French twice and the Spanish once. On the other hand, his sports car victories were more numerous. He won Le Mans, the Belgian 24 Hours, the Pescara 12 Hours, the Supercortemaggiore GP – a sports car race in spite of its title – and the Sebring 12 Hours. Moreover, of the three great drives for which he will always be remembered, namely the French Grand Prix of 1953, and Le Mans and the Tourist Trophy in 1955, two were at the wheel of a Jaguar D sports car.

In fact, even though he was World Champion, Hawthorn was probably a better sports car driver than a Grand Prix driver, though it must be remembered that Mike was out of action for some months in the 1954 season with the burns sustained at Syracuse, that in 1955 and 1956 he made the great error of signing to drive for uncompetitive British Grand Prix teams.

What is also remarkable about Hawthorn's career is the number of times he finished a Grand Prix in second or third place. It was his consistently high placings and not outright victories that gained him the World Championship. Now, a driver with this sort of record is the exact opposite of the win-or-bust driver for he is one who will conserve his car and drive to finish should victory be out of his reach. Hawthorn was consistently good with flashes of supreme brilliance when only a Fangio could hold him.

# CHAPTER EIGHT

# Jim Clark

## *by* Barrie Gill

There is a period of the four/five day mechanical melange that makes up a Grande Epreuve that has a special magic all of its own – the last half-hour of final practice. For three days drivers and mechanics, designers and tyre technicians have battled with the circuit : its surface, its corners and cambers, and its peculiar perversities. Thirty minutes remain to convince themselves and the opposition that they have mastered the challenge. Thirty minutes remain for the final modifications to be made, the right tyres to be fitted, the fuel load lightened – and for the driver to make a final, pole-seeking burst.

It is a tense, expectant time that has lost much of its gloss since April 7, 1968 – the bitter afternoon on which Jim Clark died. For no driver has ever made that 'final' half-hour such a personal monopoly. I have lost count of the number of times that I started a Grand Prix practice story with some immortal cliché like 'Jim Clark this evening grabbed pole position for tomorrow's Grand Prix with an electrifying last minute dash ... etc., etc., etc.'

It happened so often. As practice wore on Jimmy would be sitting helmetless, on the pit counter ... probably chewing his nails, and certainly keeping a far more watchful eye on rivals' times than seemed apparent. And, as you wandered down the pits an 'opposition' team manager would ask – with feigned indifference – 'Is Jimmy going out yet?' Then he would pull on the blue helmet; snuggle into the Lotus and go out and clip the vital fractions from the fastest time to date. And the journalists would go and place their transfer-charge phone calls.

It sounds theatrical. It wasn't meant to be. There was nothing theatrical about Jim Clark. He simply chose to make his supreme effort at a time that left no one a chance to supplant him. And the success of this oft-used tactic can be judged on statistics alone. In 1962, he took pole position in six out of nine Grands Prix. In 1963 his score was seven out of ten. In 1964 the count was five out of ten and in 1965 six out of ten. And in that four-year period he won no fewer than NINETEEN World Championship Grands Prix!

For pole position mattered to Jim Clark. He liked to win his races from the front – from start to finish. Graham Hill once told me : 'He changed completely when he stepped into a car. He had an aggressive, almost killer instinct in his tactics. He was scrupulously fair. He was one of the safest men you could ever wish to compete against.

'But he used to just storm away – to try to build up an enormous lead and simply try and sap your will to win by making it seem impossible. He was never happier than when he was dictating the race – from the front.'

It was a happy habit that made Jim Clark the dominant factor in Grand Prix racing from 1962 to that tragic spring day in 1968 when motor racing lost one of its greatest men. His death left a vacuum that no one has been able to fill. Stewart has the flair and Jacky Ickx has the same sort of confident ability on his day. Rindt had the speed. But not one of these men – all three of them great drivers – has provided the same sort of aura as the sheep farmer who left the borders to conquer horizons beyond his wildest dreams.

Indeed, few Champions can ever have had such placid, pastoral beginnings. Born in Fife in 1942, he moved to the now legendary Eddington Mains farm near Duns, Berwickshire when he was only six years old. With four elder sisters to rule the roost, it was perhaps not surprising that he should seek masculine solace in things mechanical : tractors, and other intriguing farming machinery. Later in life Jimmy described the advantages of having a 1,240 acre 'playground' : 'You will find few farmer's sons who don't drive from a very early age. A farm is not only littered with fascinating machinery – and I had an insatiable mechanical curiosity – but it is also private ground where driving licences don't count.'

The youthful Jimmy was quick to take advantage of these pastoral privileges. Too quick! 'First I learned to drive a tractor and then – when I was only nine – I drove my father's Austin Seven. He didn't teach me to drive. I just seemed able to remember how he had worked the controls.'

Like Graham Hill, Jim Clark had little need of instruction. But his adventuresome spirit quickly led to his first crash – at a mere ten years old. He had decided to reverse his father's latest acquisition, a cumbersome Alvis Speed Twenty out of the garage. Unfortunately he was too small to reach the pedals *and* see out of the windscreen. And during his jack-in-the-box manoeuvring he caught his sleeve in the hand throttle and charged into a very solid brick wall.

'It was my first shunt,' confessed Jimmy. 'And it was years before I dared to tell anyone about it.'

Jimmy even earned his first driving fee on the family farm – piloting a tractor from stook to stook for sixpence an hour. He loved the farm and despite a public school education at Loretto – quit school at sixteen to become a shepherd back at Erdington Mains. But though Loretto hadn't instilled much enthusiasm for Latin into the strong-minded Clark, it had kindled his interest in motor racing. He read the school library's three motor racing books from cover to cover and was taken to a race meeting at Brands Hatch by relatives.

He said later : 'I found it very exciting indeed. But I certainly didn't feel involved. After all, if you watch a lion-tamer at a circus you never dream that one day you will be in the cage yourself!'

He was certainly not to receive any family encouragement to become a motor sport enthusiast. His father wouldn't let him have a motor-bike but he did pass on his Sunbeam Talbot to Jimmy – when he passed his test just six weeks after reaching his 17th birthday. And it wasn't long before Jimmy decided to enter his first competitive event : a debut that rankled with him for the rest of his life. He entered for a driving test meeting organised by the Berwick and District Motor Club – and won. But he was then declared ineligible because he was not a member of the Club. He didn't, however, let his initial disappointment deter him from entering more and more events – despite his father's furrowed brows when he realised that Jimmy's car was costing five times as much to run as any of the other family vehicles!

Scottish budgets notwithstanding, Jimmy was now to embark on the sort of amateur apprenticeship which is a unique feature of British motor sport life. It is not mere co-incidence that has unearthed Champion after Champion from these overcrowded islands. There is an invaluable network of enthusiasm and endeavour that allows any licensed Briton to try his hand at some sort of motoring competition – be it treasure hunt, local rally, club racing or any of the hundred or so events that typify every British week–end.

And Jimmy was to qualify at all levels. Together with the friend who was to encourage him throughout his career, Ian Scott Watson, Jimmy started rallying. After failing miserably as a navigator (through reading the map backwards!) Jimmy settled into the driving seat.

The rest of the story is legend. Ian Scott Watson is one of those rare people who will sacrifice self. He recognised Jimmy's superior skill without a twinge of envy. He had no hesitation on handing his car over to Jimmy and from that moment was to push and push until Jimmy found himself at the top – almost despite himself. In 1956, Ian Scott Watson loaned Jimmy his DKW for a sports car race – and Jimmy finished last! But he had got the taste. Despite family opposition – and he had to race in secret far enough away from his family home for it to pass unnoticed – he was raring to have another go. His first love was still farm work, and he hadn't given motor racing a thought as a career – but the die was cast.

After winning four sprint events in the DKW and in his sunbeam, Jimmy was really 'blooded' when he drove a big Porsche – which had once belonged to sporting bandleader Billy Cotton – in a Border Motor Racing Club meeting at Charter-hall. And scored his first race win.

It was not a popular achievement as far as his family were concerned. As the only son, Jimmy was continually made aware of his responsibilities. But other eyes were aware of his extra-ordinary, natural driving ability. The Scottish Border Reivers team had decided to race again and, having purchased a superb Jaguar D Type, they asked young Jimmy to race for them in 1958. As far as Jimmy was concerned: 'I was being dropped in at the deep end. I would probably have preferred to start racing with a smaller car – but there is no doubt that

it was the best thing that could have happened to me. I
learned to handle power. And I learned to drive "within myself" – within my capabilities.'

It was an essential lesson. For the Border Reivers' ambitions
knew no bounds. In April 1958, Jimmy found himself on the
forbidding Spa circuit in the Belgian pine forests – matched
against contemporary heroes like Archie Scott-Brown and
Masten Gregory. It was to be a tragic first foreign race for the
young Clark. Archie Scott-Brown was killed. For the first time
the grimmer side of racing had caught up with Jimmy. But it
was still only a hobby. He continued to rally, to sprint and
to hill-climb. And by December the team had decided to 'go
single-seater' – and try Formula Two. Jimmy tested a Lotus at
Brands Hatch – under the stern eyes of Colin Chapman – but
lost interest when he saw Graham Hill lose a wheel and crash
a few minutes later.

Formula Two was not going to have another recruit as far
as Clark was concerned! How strange to think that Graham
Hill's crash might have prevented him from having to tangle
with Clark during those incredible later years when between
them they dominated Grand Prix racing?

But Jimmy's Brands Hatch excursion was not entirely fruitless. He tested a Lotus Elite and liked it as much as he hated
the Formula Two car. And he jumped at the chance to race
one at the famous Brands Hatch Boxing Day meeting. It was
a historic occasion. For Clark, the man who was to establish
Lotus as World Champions, spent the afternoon dicing with
Lotus chief Colin Chapman. Colin won – and frequently mentioned it in later years!

Jimmy meanwhile stayed with Border Reivers and Jaguars,
campaigning in a Lister-Jaguar in 1959. He was now to find
himself mixing with the 'big boys' – finishing second to
Graham Hill at Aintree and dicing with Ron Flockhart at
Silverstone. And in June, he was teamed with John Whitmore
in a Lotus Elite at Le Mans. They finished tenth. But the
turning point for Jimmy was the Goodwood TT in August. The
twenty-two-year-old sheep farmer was invited by Ecurie Ecosse
to share the wheel of their Tojeiro-Jaguar with no less a star
than the American Masten Gregory. It was to be a very
significant race indeed.

Like every sportsman, Jimmy had heroes and targets. Masten was one of his heroes. But he found he could drive just as quickly as Masten – and it was, perhaps, the first time he really began to think seriously about his ability.

This will come as no surprise to anyone who knew Clark in the later years. He often took a lot of convincing about many things but once he had made a judgment, it was often unswerving. Jimmy now knew he was a driver. He was infected by the sheer fun of driving, and the strongest parental opposition couldn't deter him.

The next chapter really belongs to one of the most astute men in motor racing – big Reg Parnell. His untimely death through illness robbed motor sport of one of its most far-seeing and most kindly 'father figures'. I often hear people refer to the part Reg played in bringing Chris Amon to Britain; in encouraging John Surtees to try his luck at four wheels, but few people seem to remember that it was Reg who first recognised *and acted upon* the potential of the slight Scotsman. He was the first man to offer Jimmy a Formula One drive – for the Aston Martin team in 1960. And when Jimmy refused a single-seater chance – because he didn't feel competent – Reg persevered and invited him to try his hand at Goodwood.

It was a bitter day. There was frost in the air and ice on the track. And Jimmy was once again thrown in at the deep end. Reg decided to turn the heat on with a few laps in the brutal 4.2-litre Aston Martin DBR2 sports car. Jimmy soon found that he could handle the car, and a Formula One Aston rolled out. Like his friends and rivals, Graham Hill and Jackie Stewart, Jimmy was to gain an everlasting impression from his first real drive in a powerful single-seater. He was confident enough to return to Goodwood for a second trial. Again, he enjoyed driving the Aston, and agreed to join the Formula One team. Much to the annoyance of Colin Chapman who had exactly the same idea in mind for the Scotsman he had defeated at Brands.

Jimmy's nine victories in the Lotus Elite in 1959 – in between piloting the big Lister-Jaguar – had not gone unnoticed in the Lotus camp. And as soon as Jimmy had finished testing the Aston for Reg, Mike Costin of Lotus wheeled on a Lotus Formula Junior. Jimmy was astonished at the leech-like handling and made two decisions at once : to drive in Grand Prix for Reg and Aston Martin and Formula Junior and Formula Two for Lotus and Colin Chapman.

The sheep farmer had decided to try his hand at racing in earnest. And on March 19th at Goodwood, Clark J. lined up for the first time in Team Lotus colours. It was a dream début. He set a new lap record, had a tremendous duel with John Surtees and gained his first Formula Junior victory – and scored the first of a host of victories for Team Lotus. From that moment on his career began to accelerate at a giddy pace. He went on to win Formula Junior races at Oulton Park, Goodwood again, and Silverstone. And in June looked forward to driving in his first Grand Prix for Astons at Zandvoort.

But Reg's team ran into qualifying trouble and withdrew. And Colin Chapman didn't need any prompting to give Jimmy his Grand Prix début in one of HIS cars instead. It was a momentous occasion. Clark settled confidently but cautiously into the $2\frac{1}{2}$-litre Lotus Climax and drove with his head. After only fifteen laps he was lying sixth and the Dutch crowd were privileged to be the first of millions to be thrilled by a duel between Clark (Lotus) and Hill (BRM). Regrettably a broken gearbox left the matter unsettled – but Clark and Hill were to dispute their skills at high speed for many a year to come.

Fourteen days later, Clark was again to take John Surtees' place in the Lotus G.P. team – while John did battle on two wheels elsewhere. It was the Belgian Grand Prix at Spa – and once again the forbidding Ardennes circuit was the scene of bitter tragedy. In practice, Clark was unnerved by two crashes involving Lotus cars. First, Stirling Moss smashed both his legs in a 130 mph accident at Burneville, and then Michael Taylor was hospitalised when the steering of his Lotus broke. The race itself was to provide two fatalities. Clark had the sickening experience of watching Chris Bristow's body being dragged from his path and laps later Alan Stacey, Jim's teammate, was killed when a bird flew in his face.

Jimmy was never inclined to be overdramatic or sensational, but he was deeply shocked by these two accidents. He said later : 'If I had seen the second accident as well as the Bristow one, I'm sure I would have retired from racing there and then. When I finished the race, my car was spattered with blood. I didn't want to know about another motor race.'

Of course, time covered the wounds – even if the scars never vanished. Jimmy explained in his more relaxed and trusting moments how he was 'blessed with a convenient memory. I can often put the sad and serious memories away while I concentrate on the next race and the problems of the present.'

But he never forgave Spa for those two, unhappy, first visits. Jimmy was rarely a man to join in 'union' grumbles about circuits. He once told me : 'I don't understand what all the fuss is about. A circuit isn't meant to be easy. They're meant to test you.' But Spa was different. Even after winning three Belgian Grands Prix in succession – including his first G.P. win in 1962 – he was bitter about 'its lack of safety. It just doesn't give you a chance if something goes wrong'.

He never forgot the bird incident either. At Rheims in 1965 he was struck in the eye by a bird, just as Alan Stacey had been. His eye was hurt, but he wasn't injured otherwise. Two years later a bird smashed into his car at Spa itself – just inches from his face. He said thoughtfully : 'There's nothing you can do to prevent it. There's nothing anyone can do to prevent it. There's nothing anyone can do – but it doesn't make you feel any better !'

Fortunately there were happier incidents in 1960 to feed the convenient Clark memory. He went to Le Mans with his old team, Border Reivers, to challenge the might of Ferrari together with Roy Salvadori in a 3-litre Aston Martin. It was one of the last true amateur triumphs for Jimmy. The car was certainly not in pristine condition. The pit crew mainly comprised an irreverent but enthusiastic gang of border farmers. They were on holiday and Jimmy certainly preserved the festive mood.

He won the legendary Le Mans sprint to the cars and the Aston was first away. Despite torrential rain, Roy and Jimmy split the Ferraris – finishing third, to prevent the Maranello cars taking all first seven places. It was a fun race. But Grand Prix racing was the serious business. And Jimmy showed he meant business by scoring his second successive fifth place in the French Grand Prix. He was third in the Portuguese Grand

Prix at Oporto and he and Trevor Taylor shared the Formula Junior Championship for Lotus.

1960 had committed Jim Clark not only to racing but to Colin Chapman and Team Lotus. A partnership was being forged which was to give British motor racing some of its greatest glories. Not that 1961 was to see the start of them. This was Ferrari year as far as Grand Prix racing was concerned. Whilst British constructors seemed to be arguing and doodling about the new $1\frac{1}{2}$-litre Formula, Enzo Ferrari's designers were perfecting a 120 degree V6 1500 cc engine to supplement the already competitive 60 degree V6.

Britain's cars were in for a beating. The Jack Brabham/ Cooper Climax monopoly was over. Phil Hill, Wolfgang von Trips, Richie Ginther, Olivier Gendebien and Giancarlo Bahetti were the men to beat: because they had the new-engined Ferraris.

With a 30 horsepower handicap, only the supreme artistry and the impertinent tactics of Stirling Moss gave Britain anything to cheer during the whole of the European season. Or at least, that's the impression the general public had.

There were few headlines for Jim Clark. Yet at Zandvoort, in May, he drove what must surely rank as one of the greatest and pluckiest races of his career. The Ferraris filled the front row of the grid, with Phil Hill a shade faster than von Trips and Richie Ginther in practice. Jimmy was only tenth fastest. But the race itself was a very different affair. For the first time, Jim Clark made the most casual observer sit up and take notice. Von Trips smoked away into a lead he was never to surrender. But the heat of the battle lay behind him. Jim Clark grabbed third place behind Phil Hill and von Trips by lap five. On lap seven, still with very weighty fuel tanks, he clocked the fastest lap of the race. Three laps later he was snapping at Phil Hill's exhausts. By lap twenty-two he had squeezed by. The Ferrari pits were aghast. The crowd were delighted. Clark held Hill at bay as they duelled wheel to wheel for three laps. Hill regained second position and Clark snatched it back again.

It was a classic struggle – and only when the Lotus' handling became erratic as the fuel tanks lightened did Clark concede defeat and wisely settle for third place. But his drive had been a revelation. Even Stirling Moss's father, who had had to be content to see his son finish fourth, rushed over to congratulate the young Scot. The gentle shepherd had really bared his teeth. The 'tiger' was there for all to see.

It was tragic that such a significant drive should have been forgotten in the gloom and recrimination of Monza. In one of the saddest Grand Prix in history, Wolfgang von Trips and fourteen spectators were killed. As Clark and Von Trips headed into the notorious curvetta, Trips' Ferrari touched Clark's front wheel. Both cars spun and the Ferrari ploughed into the spectator-lined fence. Nobody in his right mind would blame Jim Clark. But in Italy emotion often leaves logic unheard. Significantly – just a few days before the race – von Trips had described Jim Clark as 'the fairest driver in Grand Prix racing today'. Every driver within view of the accident was convinced that Clark was totally free from blame. But it was a cross he had to bear for many, many years. Even on the day he became World Champion!

To brighten the legal gloom, Team Lotus scored their first ever Championship success in the US Grand Prix at Watkins Glen in October. Jimmy was seventh with a slipping clutch but the 50,000 crowd saw Innes Ireland win his – and Lotus' – first Grand Prix in fine style. The Ferrari spell had been broken after five victories in the previous seven races. And someone else had done it besides the now legendary Moss.

But Stirling's victories in the Monaco and German Grand Prix, when he outdrove the whole Ferrari fleet, had made him a world hero. And in Britain he was idolised. No wonder motor-racing held its breath when he crashed at Goodwood in 1962 – and left a gaping hole in his country's ambitions. It was an accident that would have immense significance for two men : Graham Hill and Jim Clark. Someone had to wear the Moss mantle. And the duels between the two friends – two skilled and determined men who had been waiting in the wings, unsung and unheralded – were to provide a glittering Grand Prix period.

Britain's V8 Coventry Climax was now ready. And Colin Chapman's genius was to provide it with a worthy vehicle. At Zandvoort, every driver, team manager, designer and pressman crowded round the Lotus 25. A new era of racing cars had arrived. And Jim Clark found himself lying down in the aerodynamic monocoque, getting a worm's eye view of the track.

Clutch trouble left Clark in ninth place in the new car at Zandvoort but at Spa – the circuit of such sad memories – he was to prove both his and the car's potential beyond all doubt. From fifth place on the grid, Jimmy took the lead on lap nine and was never displaced. He won by 44.1 seconds; averaged 133.8 mph and set a new lap record.

Jimmy repeated this winning form at Aintree, and few victories gave him more pleasure than this first Grand Prix win in front of a home crowd. It also gave rivals, press and public their first taste of a Clark start-to-finish victory. Jimmy was determined to get away from everyone from the start – and he did. He led for every one of the 225 miles. And he set a new lap record – just for a bonus.

The world had seen the true Clark at last. And it is worth dwelling on this first sample of a start-to-finish success. Every driver has his own approach to a race. Jim Clark's was simplicity itself : 'Murder them from the start.'

Again and again we saw him rocket off to an immediate lead, leaving the other driver's gasping behind. It must be the most disheartening sight in any driver's experience to see a rival vanish into the distance – full tanks and all – the moment the flag falls.

Incredibly, he often used to clock his fastest lap during that early burst, despite the extra weight and the scarcely scrubbed tyres. Then he would slow slightly, give the others a glimpse of hope, then force himself to speed up again to rub in his advantage unmercilessly. What was his secret? Perhaps Jimmy was just 'switched on' more quickly, intensely and completely than his rivals. During his early victories, some critics described his tactics as sheer lunacy. I have heard many a rival claim that 'Jimmy seems to go berserk when the flag falls.'

In time they were to realise that the dropping of the flag was adrenalin to Clark, the signal to switch on all his physical and mental sharpness at peak revs. He thrived on the smell of competition. And 1962 was competitive in the extreme.

Hill won at Zandvoort, Nürburgring and Monza. Jimmy won in Belgium, Britain and at Watkins Glen.

Suddenly the South African Grand Prix organisers found themselves hosts to a cliff hanging Championship Final as a post-Christmas plus. If Jimmy could win it, he was Champion. If he didn't – the title was Graham's.

I was privileged to spend the period before the race in the company of both Clark and Hill – at the parties; the Rand Grand Prix and the endless succession of barbecues. At Deal's hotel I was in the next room to Jimmy – shamefacedly preparing the Graham Hill column for the *Daily Herald* in case he won. Time and again Jimmy would pop in to 'Check what you're saying about me.'

There was no bitterness in the rivalry. There was a respect and friendship between the two combatants, that the outside world could never appreciate. Cassius Clay and Joe Frazier could have learned much from their sporting banter.

At a Durban swimming pool, Graham challenged Jimmy to a 'drowning contest – to see who could stay under the water longest. Jimmy – a hopeless swimmer – agreed . . . if Graham would go first! When someone warned Graham that he could burn under the cloudy, but nevertheless hot, sky – Jimmy volunteered : 'Don't you believe him Graham. If you could burn under cloud, everyone in England would be sunburnt all the time !'

On this same trip, a gang of us went out to dinner. A rather mercenary member of the party, with a warped wallet, left me with the bill. Saying cheerfully : 'The press will pay.' Little did he know the *Daily Herald*'s likely reaction to an £18 dinner bill ! I was more than a little worried until Jimmy came back into the restaurant, pressed a bundle of Rand into my hand and said : 'You're not being stuck with all that !' So much for Scottish meanness !

The race is, of course, part of motor racing folklore. Jim Clark shot into an immediate lead – and had built up a massive 27 second margin before a puff of blue smoke on the 59th lap marked the end. A tiny metal plug had worked loose inside the engine. Graham won the race and the Championship. And Jim Clark proved himself a great loser.

He excelled himself at the victory party : 'Before this season began,' he said, 'we knew that it was vital for BRM to win something if they were to stay in racing. We all WANTED them to win SOMETHING. But this is ridiculous!'

Jimmy also showed a fine character, in retrospect – when he mulled over the technical knockout and the lost title. 'I honestly think that Graham made a better Champion at that time than I would have done. He was better prepared for all the public activities that are so important if a Champion is really going to help the sport.'

But there was little doubt in Jimmy's mind that next year he would not be content with second best.

1963 was to be Jim Clark's year. For the first time the British public were treated to the sight of Clark cornering on three wheels in the freshly announced Lotus Cortina. The American public were to get their first, highly significant, look at Clark at Indianapolis. And the record book was to show that for the first time in history, a driver won seven World Championship Grands Prix.

Jimmy monopolised the Formula One season with twelve wins in the twenty Formula One races he entered – and victories in the Belgian, Dutch, French, British, Italian, Mexican and South African Grands Prix. Yet the result that sticks in most people's memory is a defeat – second place in his first attempt at Indianapolis! The dollar-laden American classic – the 'brickyard' circus – offered a challenge that Colin Chapman couldn't resist. He flung his lightweight rear-engined Lotus-Ford into the arena, to challenge the traditional dominance of the front-engined, 400 bhp Offenhausers.

To the amazement of the massive and partisan crowd, the Scotsman in the European car finished second. Parnelli Jones brought an Offenhauser home first, despite an oil leak twenty laps from the end. There was a lot of controversy. Many people with nothing better to do argued that the American should have been black-flagged. Jimmy himself stayed out of it. He gambled that the American car wouldn't finish the race – and was wrong. But he wasn't going to make an all-out, do-or-die effort on the oil-covered track. 'I simply reckoned it was better to finish on the track in second place than to crash off the track completely.'

But for his – and Chapman's personal satisfaction – Jimmy

returned to America. And beat the American cars at Milwaukee, lapping every driver but A. J. Foyt. The revolution had struck. Every American designer had been proved out of date. And the greatest tribute to Chapman and Clark is that every 'Indy' car was to look like a Lotus before very long. It could have been an unpleasant experience for the Americans, but Clark's total lack of bombast and his obvious, inborn, skill made it easier for the traditionalists to swallow.

Of course, Clark was to win Indianapolis – and win it well – in the Lotus 38 in 1965. But by that time he was racing against a host of similar cars. And to complete the story – his great rival Graham Hill went on to make it a British double with a storybook 'Rookie' win the following year.

1964 was a difficult year for Jimmy. He was embroiled in publicity beyond his control. He was bitter about the treatment he had received when he had won his deserved title in Monza in 1963. The Italian police had soured the whole day by interrogating the new Champion about the two year old von Trips incident.

It was a cruel way to destroy the glitter of the new crown. And, in Jimmy's opinion, the press compounded the offence by their long-running treatment of the story. Jimmy could never appreciate that to the Fleet Street editors a Champion faced with the threat of imprisonment was a better story than the world's fastest driver finally clinching the title that had obviously been his for most of the season. The hard-fought victories seemed formalities to the outsiders. The police story was news.

England's soccer Captain, Bobby Moore, must have harboured the same sort of thoughts during the 1968 World Cup 'bracelet' affair. But in 1964 sportsmen weren't the masters of the media that they seem to be now. Graham Hill was the exception rather than the rule. Jim Clark found that interviews were difficult, and was suspicious of many, many pressmen. There could have been no greater contrast than between the Scot who held the title in 1963 and the Scot, Jackie Stewart, who held it in 1969. Jimmy never lost his dislike of being quizzed on personal matters. He knew he was famous. He enjoyed being recognised. He drilled himself to cope with the media. But he was offhand without exception to strangers who tried to interrogate him on matters which he felt were his business alone.

But he was never a dour, colourless man. In company that he trusted and in circumstances that permitted, he could be as wild as the next one. Few Champions can have slipped a disc snowballing! Clark did in a turbulent celebration at Cortina.

Few Champions can have burst into a highland dance at a barbecue party in a remote New Zealand. Clark did. And few Champions can have risked their neck hitched to the back of a high spirited 'trotter' (appropriately named 'Regal Scot'). Clark did.

Once established as THE man to beat, he began to live life to the full. He was never flamboyant. But he was never dull either. He played hard when the opportunity arose.

I shall not remember Jim Clark chiefly for the inevitable victories that came his way in Grand Prix in Europe, but rather for the Jim Clark I travelled with throughout the Tasman Series of 1967. Away from the disciplines and drama of the World Championship – touring in a mini-circus – that comprised Jackie Stewart, Denny Hulme, Frank Gardner, Bill Bryce, Eoin Young and myself – Jimmy showed himself in his true colours. It was a cheerful, exhausting two months of flying, fishing, water skiing, parties, golf, riding, press conferences, radio shows and sunbathing and almost every week-end – a Tasman Championship race.

Every race day, Jimmy was raring to go. He took the title in an elderly car with just two mechanics and a trailer to help. But his victories were not the real guide to his character, though again and again they underlined his sheer skill. We were more impressed with the man : a rounder character who was living life to the full. I will never forget the hilarious cricket match at Chris Amon's home – with Jimmy determined to win despite Virginia Parnell's dubious scoring; the flight in the nose of an insect spraying plane; the jet boats; the golf matches on a course where hot springs appeared with every divot.

If only the world at large could have seen him amusing three little New Zealand boys who recognised him in a village drug store. Or seen the exuberance of a 'pirate battle' on precarious little boats in the middle of a lake. Or proving his control in a power boat. It may sound boyish and boisterous. It probably was. But Jim Clark had earned his fun. He had battled with parental opposition to prove himself the fastest driver of his day. He had won the World Championship twice and conquered the fresh territory of Indianapolis.

He had never been afraid to take up any challenge. His saloon car driving was as spectacular as his Grand Prix successes. At the peak of his fame he risked his reputation in the RAC Rally and proved that, like Stirling Moss, he could have excelled in that sport too.

He was exiled to France but never forgot Scotland and the farm. He was courted on all sides but never forgot his friends. He was hounded by the less scrupulous press – but could talk with ease to those he trusted. He broke record after record – but still preferred to talk about farming. His death in an insignificant race at Hockenheim on April 7th 1968 – stunned the motor racing world. In a sport only too accustomed to tragedy, this was a body blow. It simply couldn't happen to Jimmy.

The sport still hasn't recovered from the blow. For a certain generation it will never be quite the same again. The solace can be found in the statistics – for they revive memories of victories in buccaneering style. And remind us of a man who chose to leave the tranquillity of sheep farming to prove himself in the most testing sport of all.

Eventually, tragically, he proved as vulnerable as the rest. But we are not here to make judgments on motor racing. I can only repeat the words I wrote a week after his death. For nothing can convince me that they still don't apply :

'How do you measure a life? Jim Clark could have been a successful farmer – known to a small circle. Doing a useful job well in a comparatively small society. Instead a teenage attempt at a driving test in a Sunbeam in 1955 proved to be the start of a career in which he outshone everyone who had gone before.

'Hundreds of thousands marvelled at, and revelled in, his skill right round the globe – Japan, South Africa, America and Australia. Millions saw his genius via a satellite when he shattered all logic and tradition in his little rear-engined car at Indianapolis. Schoolboys by the thousand found adventure and example in his exploits.

'He gave much to a world stultified by red tape and welfare. He wove dreams for the traffic-bound business-men. He was a charioteer and a cavalier in a mechanised world that demanded and received precision, patience and perfection.

'He had hours of glory, days of travel and years of rich experience. Who is to say that life must be measured solely by its span and its ending – and not by its fullness and fulfilment?'

# CHAPTER NINE

# Jack Brabham

## *by Alan Brinton*

*Alan Brinton, who describes himself as 'a fugitive from Fleet Street' – the* News Chronicle *disappeared from underneath him in 1960 – graduated to motoring journalism after seven years of political writing. A good grounding, those years in the Houses of Parliament, he says, because in motoring it is essential to know left from right! In recent years has freelanced in the motoring field, writing and broadcasting, and also editing the now defunct and much-lamented* Motor Racing *monthly. He makes his annual forays round the European Grand Prix 'circus' from a very appropriate base at Brands Hatch, where he is publicity manager for Brands Hatch and the other Grovewood race circuits. He is inevitably involved in motor racing of all types all round the calendar, but says his enthusiasm for the sport is still undimmed, along with his admiration for the drivers whose exploits make it possible. He is proud to rank Jack Brabham as one of his closest and most loyal friends.*

Only once do I recall seeing Jack Brabham blush. And he did in public in London's Savoy Hotel, just five weeks after he had announced his retirement from the cockpit at the end of the 1970 Mexican Grand Prix.

To a lush banquet in his honour, organised by Ford, had come a remarkable cross-section of international motor racing, past and present. World Champion drivers, motoring journalists, representatives from firms who had helped him throughout his career, the President of the CSI, some of his mechanics, his wife and eldest son, his 76-year-old father who had flown from Australia, old friends, old rivals . . . and many more.

It was the most remarkable gathering of motor racing personalities ever gathered together in one room. And as the red-coated toastmaster announced Jack Brabham, OBE, everyone in the room spontaneously stood and clapped the shy Australian.

He reddened with pleasure and over his face passed a look of near surprise. For though John Arthur Brabham had often known the adulation of race fans during 23 years in motoring competition he had surely never realised until then just what his impact had been and how much he was respected by admirers and rivals alike.

Then, under the harsh lights of the filming cameramen this 44-year-old, who never believed in opening his mouth unless he had something to say, opened the floodgates of his memory and reminisced enthrallingly to an audience hanging on his every word. It was as though the barriers were down at last and nearly a quarter of a century of self-discipline had been breached. The genial mask of taciturnity gave way to the richness of memory, and his appreciative audience felt this was a new Brabham.

In some ways it was, for behind the constant smile was a sadness that he was giving up what he loved most doing. Yet he had chosen to hang up his helmet while still at the top for those he loved – his wife Betty and their three sons. He felt he was driving just as well as ever, as indeed he had shown throughout the 1970 season, when he won the South African Grand Prix and was cruelly robbed of victory on the last lap of both the Monaco and British Grands Prix. The day before this farewell banquet he had shown his prowess round Brands Hatch, in a last demonstration in his Brabham BT33, lapping on a wet track quicker than anyone achieved during the whole day's racing. There, too, he was privately staggered by the reception of the spectators. 'They really seem to like me,' he told me during the afternoon.

And so they did, and indeed always had, from those early days fifteen years earlier when he had come to Britain 'for a season' and delighted race fans with his back-end-out cornering technique that had been nurtured on cinder tracks in Australia.

He achieved an outstanding popularity without ever trying.

For him there was seemingly never any need of a behind-the-scenes public relations expert. His answer to those who urged upon him that he would do even better if he was 'promoted' was always short and very much to the point. He would reply, 'The best way of getting on is winning races. It's results that count.' So he got the results, eschewed publicity . . . and gained friends the world over.

It was, though, his thorough dedication and preoccupation with his racing that caused him to play his cards close to his chest. As Graham Hill so rightly said at that farewell banquet, Jack was a wily old fox, both on and off the circuit. During the latter end of the 1965 season, with the new 3-litre formula in the offing, he told persistent journalists: 'Looks as though I'll have to pull out next year,' while back in Australia the Repco company were building for him V8 engines which were to give him his third world championship in 1966. The shrewd engineer in him told him he was probably on to a good thing, but why should he tell the opposition in advance?

His 1970 retirement wasn't his first. Bowing to family pressure, he had given up once before, after six years of midget racing, but that didn't last long, and from hill-climbing success he moved to road racing, and the path that was to lead him to Europe and fame.

During his long competition career he was amazingly free from serious accidents. His most alarming experience was during a test session at Silverstone in 1969 when he thumped into a bank on the far side of the circuit, probably because of a deflating tyre. He was trapped in his car and all alone, with fuel dripping perilously near to the hot exhausts. Should he press the built-in fire extinguishing system to prevent a potential fire, or wait for the flames and then press the button? He decided to press first, but it was an agonising decision that still brings a tense look as he remembers it. He had broken a bone in his foot and was out of the French Grand Prix, yet three weeks later, one leg encased in plaster, he drove an automatic transmission Zodiac up to Silverstone to watch the British Grand Prix and give all the help he could to his then team-mate, Jacky Ickx.

This determination to be back on the job was typical of his whole career. He could never sit back, never relax, and refused to entertain any thought of giving up until he was ready.

Was this Silverstone shunt the trigger which fired off thoughts of retirement? 'No,' he told me. 'I've always realised motor racing is a dangerous game, but that accident was a one-off that I hoped would not happen again. I've always felt it necessary to treat my racing with respect, and in that way the chances of survival are far higher.'

In fact, by the end of 1969 he had decided that the time had come for retirement. He wanted to be fair to Betty, who had inevitably suffered many moments of worry through the years, and he wanted to concentrate on the businesses he had been building up in preparation for a second career.

The linch-pin was whether he could get Jochen Rindt, who had driven for him in 1968, back into the Brabham team. Negotiations continued for some time, but in the end Jochen joined Gold Leaf Team Lotus, and Jack decided to do one more year.

It was a busy year and a disappointing one, for though it began with an impressive domination of the South African Grand Prix, there followed those heart-breaking last-lap failures at Monaco and Brands Hatch, mechanical failures in other world championship events and a frightening incident when he thumped a guard rail at Monza. Jack would so much have liked to have bowed out with a fourth world championship, but at least he won his penultimate race – the Paris 1000 Kilometres at Montlhery in a Matra – and was chosen (before he announced his retirement) as Driver of the Year by the Guild of Motoring Writers.

As the season progressed and he saw his chances slipping away, Jack's demeanour never changed, and neither did his determination to win the next race. After all, he had known disappointment many times before, and his victory in the French Grand Prix at Rheims in 1966 – which made history, for he was the first driver to win a Grand Prix in his own car – had come after six years without a Grand Prix success. He could always shrug off any frustration and throw himself into the highly skilled science-cum-art of 'sorting' his car to beat the opposition next time.

All the experts agree that the world has known no better developments driver than Jack. Many drivers can come into the pits and say they don't like the handling of their car, but few of them can explain exactly what is happening, and very few indeed know what must be done to effect a cure. Jack was one of those elite few, and there is no doubt that his success on circuits such as Brands Hatch, which calls for supreme handling qualities, was largely due to this ability. It was a skill that came through a blend of immense experience and engineering expertise. That was part of the reason for the devotion he always inspired from his mechanics; they knew that anything he asked them to do he could do just as well, or probably better. Trying to talk to him in his glass-fronted office at the Brabham racing shop was almost impossible; he would always be saying, 'Excuse me a moment' and going out to explain to one of his staff that something should be done another way.

In his earlier days he did a great deal of the work on his cars, and it was not at all rare to find him even towards the end of his career working at a lathe.

He had that facility for application that was almost frightening. I remember a Formula Two race just outside Brussels many years ago, when Jack arrived late on the scene because of cross-Channel fog, and asked me what the circuit was like. I did my best to describe it, but before long we were out in an Anglia which I had brought over from the Ford test fleet, touring the circuit for lap after lap until around midnight. The next day he was dissatisfied with his car's performance, and so, until the early hours of race morning he was working alongside his mechanic in the transporter in a Brussels square. It would be a nice touch to be able to report that he won the race . . . and he did just that!

There must be a spirit of adventure in all top racing drivers, and Jack had that a-plenty. There is also more than a touch of curiosity in his make-up. One day at Rheims, while still learning to fly under the tutelage of the late Ron Flockhart, he suddenly asked, 'Which do you think is quicker round this circuit – the Cessna or the Cooper?' Within minutes we were out at the airfield, the Cessna was warmed up, and soon we were flying over the famous triangular course, following as closely as possible its outlines, and Jack satisfied himself that the Cooper had the beating of his single-engined plane.

Since those days he has flown thousands of miles, including two light-plane crossings of the Atlantic and a flight to Australia. He loves his flying and is recognised as a top pilot, with the same instinctive engineer's feel for an aircraft as for a car, and the same respect for the dangers involved. He has known some tricky moments in planes – like force-landing in a field during a snowstorm and having to explain to the farmer that he wasn't trying to steal his tractor! – but in any moment of crisis he never loses his nerve, and never panics. I was sitting up front with him flying back from Pau one day, in bad visibility and receiving nothing from the navigational beacons. He nudged me surreptitiously, so that Betty would not notice. Out of the corner of his mouth, he said, 'Keep a look-out on your side and tell me if you spot the coast. At this moment we are very definitely lost.' Well, we spotted the sea, Jack was talked down by radar into Le Touquet, and Betty never learned about that particular problem until this year.

Planes interest Jack just as much as cars, and if ever he and Colin Chapman were together you could confidently bet that they were discussing flying. My pick of Jack's many flying stories is how he made a quite unauthorised and somewhat hazardous landing at a small airfield in France which shall be nameless, because one of his passengers had omitted to visit the little girls' room before they started on a four-hour flight. 'We were off again before anyone realised,' he told me with a broad grin.

Navigating a plane demands concentration and good time-keeping, but in his appointments Jack has caused me many anxious moments. During his years as builder-driver he in-evitably became the centre of a complicated series of meetings, and trying to fit them all in meant that he was invariably late almost every time. Indeed, during the whole time I've known him I can recall only one occasion on which he made a rendezvous with me spot on time ... and I was late for once. He's never let me forget it.

The first time we really got together started in Rome, when we were both on our way to the Syracuse Grand Prix, where Jack was to drive Rob Walker's Cooper. Jack had flown in from Australia and several of us were due to fly on to Syracuse. But at the airport we discovered that bad visibility over Sicily had cancelled all flights. So a bunch of us booked on a night sleeper down to Reggio Calabria, had a splendid meal on the train and retired to our bunks.

The next morning we awoke to find the train stopped, along with several others, in a station many miles from Reggio. There had been a landslide further down the line. Harry Schell, fluent in Italian as in several other languages, routed Jack and I out of the train and told us he had organised a taxi. We had a tense ride in this antiquated vehicle with the elderly Italian driver determined to demonstrate that he was a racing aficionado and not at all put out as Jack and Harry changed a wheel after the inevitable puncture.

Harry organised a hire car by getting the ferry captain to radio the harbour master at Messina, and there was a spanking new Fiat Millicento waiting for us on the quay as we stepped ashore. It was clear that Harry proposed to do the driving, so Jack and I humped our bags over to the car, and quick as a flash Jack dived into the back seat, piling his luggage alongside.

'What do you think you're doing?' I asked.

Jack grinned. 'Getting furthest from the accident,' he replied.

Well, we didn't have an accident, and we got to Syracuse in time for practice, but I still shudder at the thought of that mad drive, and still recall with admiration how Jack gave himself that extra bit of insurance. He never misses a trick.

But he did run out of petrol while racing. Like several times. There was once at Pescara when his car petered to a halt with a dead engine ... obligingly outside a petrol station, and he got going again with a few litres of fuel. There was that dramatic last lap in the 1959 United States Grand Prix at Sebring when, leading the race, he ran out of fuel again, coasted as far as he could and then pushed his Cooper the last 400 yards home, to finish fourth but still good enough for his first world championship. And that memorable 1970 British Grand Prix at Brands Hatch, when he bided his time, overtook Jochen Rindt and then proceeded to pull away to what looked like certain victory ... only to run short of fuel approaching the last corner on the last lap. Jochen swept past as Jack coasted slowly home in second place, and there were a few tear-stained cheeks in the grandstand. Yet a few minutes after he had walked back from his car to the pits, grim of face and clearly in the depths of despair, Jack was again his cheerful, smiling self. 'After Monaco and now this,' he said, 'I'm going to suggest that every Grand Prix should be one lap less than in the regulations.' And for that last demonstration at Brands Hatch he asked for fuel to be laid on at every marshals' post!

You must have a sense of humour to survive the bitter fortunes of motor racing, and though it was usually a private affair between close friends, Jack often leavened his many disappointments with a quip or two. But behind the smile he was always dead serious. After a frightening episode at Indianapolis, when he had to drive through a complete wall of flame, he declared he would never go there again . . . but eventually did, because he could never resist a challenge, and he desperately wanted to win there. For years he said he would never return to Le Mans . . . but went back in 1970 to drive a Matra and was the quickest in the team until his car broke. He hated the potential dangers of the ultra-fast Spa-Francorchamps circuit, especially after that first-lap fracas in the 1966 Belgian Grand Prix when half the field left the course after running into a surprise rainstorm, but he never failed to turn up on the grid there.

He was indeed a real professional, always giving of his best and never content to be just second. 'You've got to have a bit of devil in you to win races,' he once told me. 'There's got to be a streak in you that isn't quite nice, something that makes you force your way through when the opportunity presents itself.' Over the years, he felt, there weren't too many with that streak, but they were the winners.

So he could play it tough when necessary, take a calculated risk if the situation demanded it, and use a lot of grass on the corners if he thought it would help. He was not always the most elegant driver on a circuit; one of his top rivals once declared that Jack never took the same corner twice in the same way. But whether he did or not, he got the results. Impressed most vividly by the way Fangio drove through the downhill sweeps after the pits at Rouen, he did his utmost to model himself on that great Argentinian. He smoothed out his cornering style, realising that the cinder track technique was not the best for tarmac, but when under pressure that hang-out-the-tail procedure still showed right to the last season.

If Fangio was his idol, his greatest rival was undoubtedly Stirling Moss. 'Stirling,' he said, 'was the most difficult man to beat on pretty well any circuit, because he not only had the skill but he thought deeply about his racing.'

And Stirling also cultivated his public image, to a point where he could retire in a race and still get the headline. I sensed that this irked Jack, and I shall never forget his pleasure one Monday morning when I showed him a *Daily Express* front page story headed: 'Brabham fails in GP.' He really felt he had arrived!

There were two races that stand out vividly in his memory. One, very naturally, was his winning drive in the 1959 Monaco Grand Prix; his first world championship victory, and the start of his first world championship success. The other came at Rheims in the summer of 1966 when he drove his Repco-powered Brabham to win the French Grand Prix, and become the first driver to win a GP in a car he had constructed himself. The pleasure was the greater because he was using an Australian engine, but even after receiving the winner's garland he still couldn't relax; a short time later he was pressed against the rails of the paddock, eating a hunk of melon and watching the fortunes of Brabham cars in a Formula Three event.

It seems so natural that his cars should be called Brabhams, yet that is not how it began. The first car he built – a Formula Junior – was named after his firm, Motor Racing Developments, and I quietly suggested that the title MRD might well provoke some raw comment in France. Jack's knowledge of French is ... well, rudimentary, but after his car's first trip to France someone told him about that common expletive, and the name was changed. Like fast.

But if he learned at least one French word, Jack never learned to like French cooking. On the eve of a French Grand Prix at Rheims, where there was no practice on a Saturday, he flew all the way back to England 'to get a proper meal'.

He is not fussy about his food, so long as it is well-cooked steak! He says he gave up smoking when he left school, and he must have drunk enough bitter lemon to sink an aircraft carrier. Apart from his flying, his only active interest outside motor racing was skin diving, and at that, according to fellow Australian driver Frank Gardner, Jack was always inclined to be a bit too venturesome. He once bought a bag of golf clubs, intending to play on the course behind his home at Byfleet, but never found the time. (He thought it was a good suggestion to be photographed swinging a club, to be captioned, 'Learn to drive with Jack Brabham,' but somehow never found the time.)

For nearly a quarter of a century Jack Brabham, OBE, rarely found time for anything except the motor racing he loved. Those last few demonstration laps at Brands Hatch on November 29th were, he confessed, the toughest he had ever driven. When, a few minutes later, he was nearly knocked off the starter's rostrum by a car involved in a collision as it left the grid, Jack observed : 'Perhaps it would be safer to make a comeback in South Africa next March.'

But it was all over, and he knew it. The next evening, at that Ford banquet, Betty was presented with a ball and chain which carried the inscription 'You won in the end.'

And so she had.

# CHAPTER TEN

# Bruce McLaren

## by Eoin S. Young

*Eoin S. Young, born in Timaru, New Zealand, in 1939, worked for five years in a bank, six months as a reporter in the* Timaru Herald *and in 1961 came to Europe as a motor racing freelance. He toured the tracks with Denis Hulme, and in 1962 joined Bruce McLaren as his personal secretary. In 1963 he became a director of Bruce McLaren Motor Racing Ltd. In 1966 he started his own business as freelance journalist and racing consultant and now has regular columns in* Autocar *in England,* Road & Track *in America, and other magazines throughout the world.*

There have been men in motor racing who were better drivers, better engineers, better designers, and better car-builders, but there has been no one man who combined these qualities as successfully as Bruce McLaren, the New Zealander who was tragically killed in June, 1970 while test-driving the latest in a super-successful line of McLaren CanAm sports cars. He was thirty-two.

At the end of the previous season, while his team was putting finishing touches to a new car that was to run in the Indianapolis 500, Bruce McLaren went up to London to be presented with the BRDC Gold Star – the British Racing Drivers' Club's top award in international racing. He had won it in the face of opposition from Jackie Stewart, the brilliant World Champion who had completely outpaced his Grand Prix contemporaries that season. McLaren's achievements in 1969 included winning the CanAm sports car championship for the second time, and finishing third in the World Championship behind Stewart and Jacky Ickx, but he talked seriously of retiring from the Grand Prix scene to concentrate on the development of new cars.

'I would like to phase myself out of Formula One because I consider I can be either a good racing driver or a good engineer. I feel I could be a better racing driver than I am, and I could be a better engineer than I am, but I could be a better engineer than a racing driver, and I feel the company (Bruce McLaren Motor Racing Ltd) is going to be more dependent on its cars and on its engineering than it is on its drivers.'

As if to back up these engineering claims, the Indiana section of the Society of Automobile Engineers presented a special plaque to Bruce in recognition of his contribution to progress at the Speedway.

Bruce talked of retiring from Formula One, but he had no intentions of giving up CanAm sports car racing – his favourite – or development test driving which he also enjoyed since it gave him an opportunity to evaluate his own ideas on the race track in a car that had been built by his own team. It was the enjoyment of a father teaching his infant son to walk and talk.

When Jack Brabham, McLaren's mentor during his early years in Europe, announced his retirement from racing at the end of the 1970 season he was careful to say that this included retirement from test driving as well. Bruce's fatal accident weighed heavy on the consciences of thinking drivers, because of all the topliners Bruce seemed the least likely to have an accident.

Looking back through the McLaren career it appears obvious that Bruce created ambitions merely to achieve them. When he was nine years old and crippled with Perthes Disease the doctors hinted privately to his parents that he might never walk again. He did. It took him two years before he emerged from hospital on crutches, but he had won his first battle with the world. Compared with this triumph of personal mobility, all other challenges paled in significance.

His father, Les, was already a figure of note in Auckland motor sporting circles from his exploits on motor cycles, but it was his decision to buy an Ulster Austin Seven that formed the foundation of his thirteen-year-old son's future fame. Les, known to everyone in New Zealand motor racing as 'Pop' in years to come, rebuilt the Ulster from boxes of rusting bits, and doubtless looked forward to the first test run with mounting enthusiasm. He came back from the run with his hopes in tatters. The car, he said, would neither steer nor stop and he gave his young son to understand that he was about to compose a classified advertisement for the sale of this noxious vehicle just as soon as his hands stopped shaking. Bruce, a diplomat even then, pleaded his case and eventually won, since his father obviously became aware during the presentation of the case that the Ulster could be an extremely effective practical base for the engineering degree that Bruce was about to embark on.

The little 1929 Austin with its 747 cc and 24 horsepower became something of a symbol to Bruce later in his career. He talked of the early work he did on the car to make it handle and perform better as the essential first lessons for any aspiring designer of racing cars.

'I've always said that a designer who has a college degree and raced his own Austin Seven is going to be a beauty, but the guy who's just got his college degree and specialised in thermo dynamics or something, no matter how brilliant he may be in space age technology, he's just not going to get the job done in the overall area of racing cars.'

Bruce maintained that since modern engineering is tending to become so much more specialised there will be few opportunities for college graduates to get the broad base of experience to enable him to design and develop a racing car.

'He could be part of a team, but then you get this terrible committee hassle. The sort of experience that Jack Brabham and Colin Chapman and I were lucky enough to get growing up with the racing industry is very difficult to impart now that the industry is so well established. Where does a young engineer start now? Nobody races Austin Sevens any more, but Chapman did, and I did . . .'

When the Austin became too highly tuned to drive on the road (after McLaren modifications it would do 87 mph through the flying quarter-mile and a standing quarter took under 20 seconds) Bruce sold it to buy a Ford Ten Special which he could also drive to engineering college. There was never the rapport with this car that he enjoyed with the little Austin, and he looked forward more to his races in his father's modified Austin Healey 100–4. They soon came to an arrangement whereby the fastest driver in practice would race the car, and 'Pop' found himself more involved with the lap charts and stopwatches and less with the driving.

The Healey was part of his grounding as was the bob-tailed ex-Brabham 1½-litre Cooper sports car which led in short order to a deal with Brabham to bring out a 1750 cc single-seater Cooper for Bruce to drive in the 1958 New Zealand Grand Prix at Ardmore. Gearbox trouble just before the race dashed his hopes and the field had already covered half a lap when the number 47 Cooper roared round the back of the pits and into the race. The hometown crowd roared their approval as the twenty-year-old took up the chase.

Battles against the odds seemed to feature in a glance at the McLaren career. This mildest of men could summon the most prodigious efforts when roused, but it took a lot to rouse him. At Mosport in Canada leaking fuel bags in his CanAm car saw him tyre-smoking down the pit lane in pursuit of the field nearly a minute ahead. He tigered through to finish second behind team-mate Hulme in a twin McLaren. At Pukekohe, with an early Downton Cooper Mini, he was deprived of his pole position in the saloon race when drivers of bigger cars protested that they would run over the little car at the start. Enraged, Bruce drove like a man possessed, took the lead after a couple of laps and held it almost to the end when he had to slow into second place with overheating. This fierce competitive spirit was always bubbling below the surface like a dormant volcano.

He caught the field and was through to eighth place in that 1958 race when the engine started misfiring and he headed for the pits. It was a mistake bred of inexperience. The car had been warming up on the jacks when the transmission started rattling, and in the haste to change the gearbox the soft 'warm-up' spark plugs had been left in. Precious ground was eroding away as the plugs were changed and Bruce went back into the race a lonely last, deprived even of this when the oil drained out of the hastily bolted-up gearbox and he was out of the race. But the organisers of the Grand Prix were

CONCENTRATION

Bruce McLaren at the wheel of his own car. He chased Jackie Stewart home to a fine second place in the Spanish Grand Prix, Barcelona, 1969.

'HONEST KEN, IT WAS THIS BIG!'

FISHING fanatic Jackie Stewart has a likely tale to tell to team-chief Ken Tyrrell before the Spanish Grand Prix in 1969. But he did catch the 'Big One' at the end of the season—taking the Championship with ease. He also won the Spanish Grand Prix.

THE SIX FACES OF JIM CLARK
A unique, quick-fire, series of Jim Clark studies: a photographic tribute to Clark the Man: quizzical, pensive, alert and downright happy.

'MR. CONFIDENCE'

Jackie Stewart, without doubt the outstanding driver in 1971, pictured just before the start of the French Grand Prix.

RUNAWAY WINNER

Stewart en route to the victory flag—in a superb start-to-finish triumph in the French Grand Prix 1971.

aware of the effort the youngster had put in, and they awarded
him the first 'Driver to Europe' scholarship, a fund that paid
his expenses for a season's racing in England with Jack
Brabham promising to keep an eye on his interests.

In a way Jack was shepherding Bruce carefully along
eventually to place him as his 'number two' in the Cooper
Grand Prix team in 1959, as he later did with Denny Hulme
who became Jack's team driver in 1964 and was groomed for
the Grand Prix team for 1966.

Bruce discovered the way of European racing that first
season and was able to cope with the 'old pals' acts' and the
chatting-up that was necessary in European racing politics
but unknown in New Zealand. By comparison, Denny Hulme
wasn't able to handle the politics and diplomacy required
when he arrived over as 'Driver to Europe' in 1960 and his
trip to the top took a lot longer than Bruce's. McLaren was
fortunate in having a charm of manner that opened many
doors. He was the universal 'nice guy' who was so hard to dislike that he had no enemies.

In 1959, he won the American Grand Prix at Sebring. At
twenty-two, the youngest driver ever to win a world championship race. He won the Argentine Grand Prix that opened
the 1960 season and he went on that year to finish second
behind Jack in the World Championship. In only his second
year in the 'big league'.

I wrote a book on Bruce and his racing team after his death
and in it Denny Hulme looks back on Bruce's early associa-
tions with Cooper and reasons that, while he obviously had the
talent to be given the drive in the first place, he was also just
a little lucky.

'In a funny way you could compare Bruce and Cooper with
Fittipaldi stepping into the Lotus 72. A very good car with
a guy coming up having done some good races, then getting
a good car and winning a Grand Prix very early on as Bruce
did.'

It took Denny seven years to win his first Grand Prix after
he arrived in England, but he carried on during the 1967
season to win the World Championship.

With the ambition to win a Grand Prix soon achieved, the
next goal on the McLaren horizon was the World Champion-

ship – or perhaps a Grand Prix win in his own car. He was able to score the second wish but not the first. The Cooper cars lost their initial advantage in Grand Prix racing (they had benefited by being first with rear engines in the late 'fifties) when Colin Chapman pressed on with innovation and development on his Lotuses and he was to command the decade as a successful car-builder and supplier of cars to Jim Clark.

The brilliance of the McLaren star was waning with the Cooper competitiveness when the formula changed from 2½-litres to 1½-litres and Bruce decided to form his own team. At first it was set up to compete in sports car racing, a field that Bruce saw great potential in, but Coopers were not prepared to build a car for him. The first appearance of the embryo McLaren team was the 1964 Tasman series newly reorganised under a 2½-litre formula to capitalise on pensioned-off Formula One equipment. With special slimline lightweight Coopers built almost in secret in the Cooper workshops because Charles Cooper did not consider a special car was necessary for the Antipodean races, Bruce won his home series but he returned saddened by the death of his team-mate, the brilliant young American Timmy Mayer who had been killed when his Cooper hit a tree in a practice accident at Longford in Tasmania, the last race of the series.

Timmy's lawyer brother Teddy eventually joined forces with the young McLaren organisation as they embarked in a programme to build a sports car for the dollar-rich string of professional road races in America. Mayer knew the score in America and Bruce was well able to look after the European side and the combination was a success. By the end of 1965 they had built a prototype Formula One car, and when the 3-litre formula started in 1966 an advanced new Grand Prix McLaren was ready, fitted with an Indianapolis Ford V8 engine reduced in capacity. It was the first Ford in Formula One and it was a disaster, being overweight and underpowered and generally unsuitable for the 3-litre application. It weighed like an anchor on the Grand Prix hopes of the McLaren team, and it was not until Ford of Britain financed Cosworth Engineering to build an engine and make it available, that the McLaren fortunes picked up again.

Between 1966 and 1968 Bruce had tried the ill-starred Ford,

an Italian Serenissima, a BRM V8 and a BRM V12, but with the new Cosworth-Ford in 1968 he won his first Grand Prix in his own car – the Belgian at Spa. He said later that he was convinced there was more magic than engineering involved in winning a Grand Prix.

McLaren the man was a sweetly uninvolved character, as honest as the day was long, and devoted to his wife Patty, and their baby daughter Amanda, their new home near Walton-on-Thames in Surrey, and his beloved cars – in that order. He had immense mechanical sympathy. It almost seemed that he could feel what a car was trying to tell him ... the sort of relationship that exists between a top horseman and his mount. His capacity for work was staggering and his staff at the factory in Colnbrook would often arrive at work to find their boss, sleeves rolled up, puzzling over a part of the car that he was trying to improve. And even more often they would look up to see the lights burning in the chairman's office as they went home at night. Time was something that never seriously hampered McLaren activities – unless it was something that had to be rationed when a new car was reaching its completion deadline. Patty often had to phone the factory to remind her husband that not only did they have guests arriving for dinner that night – the guests were already at the door ringing the bell!

As a designer and an engineer, Bruce was able to enjoy his flights of fancy that were known in the workshops as 'Brucie's Whoosh-Bonks'. This was the favourite McLaren way of describing a car-building programme and minimising the time and difficulties involved.

'It's simple,' he would say to a vaguely disbelieving group of mechanics. 'We design it in the drawing office. That'll only take a couple of days. Whoosh! Then we get all the stuff cast up. We can bolt it together down the back of the shop. Bonk! See how simple it'll be? Whoosh-Bonk and the job's done.'

Bruce's enthusiasm was infectious and this was how he called on the 50-odd employees to greater efforts, and was able to draw talent from people who probably never realised they were capable of such work. If Bruce believed something was possible it could be done.

The first and most famous Whoosh-Bonk car was a space-frame single-seater version of the current CanAm sports car, and it really was designed by Bruce on scraps of paper as he chatted with the mechanics outlining his plans. It was to be an inexpensive car ideal for club racing, hill climbing, or sprinting. It would use all the running gear from the sports car. In fact no designs exist of this car – officially filed as the M3 – because the first chassis frames were built free-hand to Bruce's jotted specifications. Later a designer was called in to copy the design from an actual chassis while the McLaren design team pressed on with more important projects, but the Whoosh-Bonk drawings were fated. The cleaner that night thought the rolled-up drawing paper was scrap and burned it!

The CanAm sports cars were Bruce's pride and joy. He took a delight in creating them, and revelled in driving these 650-horsepower pieces of rumbling mechanical poetry. In 1967 he won the CanAm title, and he won it again in 1969. In 1968 and 1970 Denny Hulme kept the Championship in the McLaren 'family'.* In 1968 he won the Johnson Wax CanAm award almost by prior arrangement because Bruce believed in treating his team fairly. They were in such total command of the sports car series that they were taking turn-about at winning. But in 1970 Denny won the Championship for Bruce, his team-mate and close friend who had been killed testing the new 1970 M8D at the start of the season.

'Bruce really liked CanAm racing,' recalls Denny. 'It was his one big thing and it made the world of difference that he was in a CanAm car and not in a Formula One car. He'd be the hardest guy in the world to beat in a sports car, but although he probably put the same amount of effort into Formula One he didn't get the same results back out of the car. One of the reasons for this, I think, is that Bruce was so smooth. A CanAm seems to get slower if you fling it about, but I reckon the only way to get a Grand Prix car going quick is to start hurling it around and really getting it set up for fast corners. Bruce didn't like doing this, and this probably is why I was quicker in a Formula One car than he was.'

Bruce was often asked if he had plans to follow Chapman's Lotus progress and build a road car, and he would answer that when the McLaren image had been built to a suitable

* In 1971, Peter Revson took the title – to preserve the McLaren monopoly.

status through racing they would use the established name to promote a road car. His joke was that he would build a road car when someone asked Jack Brabham if he drove a McLaren. In fact another of Bruce's pet projects was a proto- type of a road car developed from a GT version of a CanAm car. He soon discovered that there were habitability problems in converting a racing car to a road-going machine, but he enjoyed showing off his personal GT. The project was shelved when Bruce was killed.

Bruce and Chris Amon won the Le Mans 24-Hour race in a Ford GT in 1966, an effort which Bruce thought was only fitting since he had helped to develop and test the Fords since the 'Win Le Mans' programme had started at Dearborn. Roy Lunn, then in charge of the Ford racing organisation, was most impressed by Bruce's combined abilities as driver and engineer in their detailed testing sessions with the Fords. 'He would come in after a test run and tell you exactly what had happened, and what's more he could tell you what to do to put it right. He was just a wonderful combination of a driver and engineer and car builder, and he could also com- municate with you. I think that was the success of his cars. He had all three, and minimum communication problems be- cause they were all locked into one guy. That was the problem we had. If we were designing and building a car, we weren't capable of driving and testing so we had to rely on the test driver to communicate back. Bruce was able to communicate back – he could tell you you had a problem and also how to cure it . . .'

Discussions with Bruce after dinner at his home were always lively and illuminating. He always had a clear-cut and vividly simple way of putting his point. I wondered once if he thought that some racing drivers were better able to combine their engineering and experience to come up with a successful car than, say, Ferrari or BRM who hired engineers to build their cars.

'No, no, no. Ferrari used to be a driver, Colin Chapman used to be a driver. Someone else could ask the same question in fifteen years time when people are saying "Remember 1969? Those were the great days when we had McLarens and Brabhams and Lotuses." And there'll be kids coming out with race cars that we've never heard of and we'll look down our noses just as other people looked down their noses at us.'

Did this mean that it was essential to have raced if you were planning to build a racing car? Was this an insurmountable hurdle for people who came 'cold' into the racing business?

'It's almost that way. How far do you want to go back? The Chevrolet brothers . . . Henry Ford used to race . . . the Maserati brothers . . . maybe there's a better chance of being good at it if you have the "feel" for racing . . . the Healeys . . . BRM. You see, Raymond Mays used to race. That's interesting. A good point. Think about that. Matra came in from the cold to start building racing cars but in fact they didn't do particularly well in Grand Prix racing until Ken Tyrrell was involved. And Ken Tyrrell used to race. . . .'

Tyrrell, a man whose word in racing Bruce respected, entered Matras for Jackie Stewart in Formula One winning the World Championship in 1969. In 1970 he switched to the new March car and eventually built his own Tyrrell-Ford car. His reputation in Grand Prix racing is that of a modern Neubauer, the legendary team manager of Mercedes and since the McLaren CanAm team has been compared to Mercedes in the thoroughness and success of their operation, the comparison is a happy one.

'The thing that impresses me most about McLarens in Can-Am racing,' says Tyrrell, 'Is not the fact that they win all the races, but the fact that they're always there when the race finishes. Our record in Formula One racing wouldn't look very bright from this angle if you compared it with the McLarens on the CanAm series.'

In addition to his complex bustling talents in racing, Bruce always was able to summarise and express comment on the racing scene for the regular columns we did together for *Autosport* and syndication abroad. When he was killed on that sunny June afternoon at Goodwood, I remembered a piece that he had taken particular pains over composing in his mind before he spoke into the tape recorder. He was numbed with the shock of Jim Clark's death at Hockenheim. 'Too often in this demanding sport, unique in terms of ability, dedication, concentration, and courage, someone pays a penalty for trying

142

to do just that little bit better or go that little bit faster. And too often someone pays the penalty just for being in the wrong place at the wrong time when a situation or set of circumstances is such that no human being can control them. However that's the way it is. We accept it, we enjoy what we do, we get a lot of satisfaction out of it, and maybe we prove something, I don't know . . .'

# CHAPTER ELEVEN

# Jackie Stewart

## *by Barrie Gill*

They call him 'the pop racing driver', 'motor sport's answer to George Best', 'Mr Professional' and 'motor racing's first millionaire'.

They have also called him World Champion – 'the Flying Scot' and 'the fastest driver in the world'. A strange assortment of titles for a diminutive, skipping Scot who was working unseen and unsung in a family garage only eight or nine years ago. But then, Jackie Stewart is a very extraordinary young man, a flamboyant yet deeply thoughtful careerist who has worked hard and hectically to earn all seven descriptions.

Jackie Stewart is a happening. A multi-dollar declaration that motor racing has finally been dragged into the entertainment world – often kicking and screaming as if it didn't know what was really good for it. In an age when a racing car costs at least £20,000 ($48,000) and it can cost up to £100,000 ($240,000) to assemble a full grid, the days of the gentlemanly amateur are over.

There is no room for a quiet, retiring violet who only wishes to arrive on race day and slip quietly away once the fanfares begin. Motor racing is the technocrats' coliseum; a knife-edge, colour-filled roaring spectacle – the fastest moving advert for the commercial giants. It's big business and it's show business. And the two claims have been the catalyst for Jackie Stewart.

Today the long-haired Scot in his way-out clothes and sponsored sun glasses has all the trappings, a sumptuous home in tax-tolerant Switzerland, a glamorous wife and two photogenic children. His friends are film stars, royalty, sportsmen and big businessmen. He has produced a record, written a book,* has a national newspaper column, makes documentaries, runs his own Speed Show, commentates, sponsors, sells, lectures, flies

* *World Champion* (Pelham).

144

400,000 miles a year and drives a racing car as quickly as any-one in the world.

Yet seven years ago – the world at large had never heard of him. John Young Stewart was 'a name' only as far as two fairly exclusive circles were concerned : the clay pigeon shooting brigade and amongst the ranks of Ecurie Ecosse followers. He was, in fact, perhaps best known as Jimmy Stewart's younger brother. For – unlike Graham Hill – Jackie had a motoring heritage. Apart from his activities in the family garage, big brother Jimmy – nine years Jackie's senior – had proved a polished and expert driver in the 'fifties until parental pressure persuaded him to retire after an accident at Le Mans.

Perhaps it was just this pressure that made Jackie choose a different sport in which to excel. He was shooting for Scotland by the time he was 17 and had won all the home champion-ships by 1960. But on his 21st birthday – his world collapsed. On the last day of the Olympic trials he suddenly went to pieces – and failed abysmally. It was to be a bitter, but life-long lesson.

He admits he had become big-headed. 'I began to think I was God's gift to shooting. I had to be firmly put in my place.'

It was an experience that has helped him maintain his equanimity in the face of some cruel disappointments in motor sport – like the time a tiny piece of gauze blocked his fuel feed and cost him his chance of the Championship in Mexico in 1968. But that's jumping the gun. Not until 1962 did Jackie turn to racing. He tested himself in private at Oulton Park. His brother set some target times and Jackie proved himself very quick indeed. The die was cast : he would drive for Ecurie Ecosse. No Graham Hill-type years in the wilderness for Jackie Stewart. Luck was on his side.

Two years later good fortune favoured him in huge chunks. Somebody mentioned his name to Ken Tyrrell, the Surrey timber merchant who had deservedly earned the reputation of 'star-maker'. At this time, the lanky Tyrrell was running the works Cooper Formula Three team. A Grand Prix team seemed as far away for him as for young Stewart. The Goodwood track manager, Robin McKay, suggested Tyrrell gave this un-known Scot a trial. Ken phoned Jackie's brother – checked to see if the lad was serious – and invited him down. That afternoon at Goodwood has passed into motor racing folklore, but it is a story that must be told in any assessment of Jackie Stewart.

The wiry youngster had never sat in a single-seater car before – and was lectured sternly by Ken Tyrrell to 'take it easy'. Bruce McLaren – already a big-name Grand Prix star – was there to do the real testing and notched up some very quick times indeed. After only three laps Stewart had equalled his time. Tyrrell called him in and lectured him again. McLaren stalked over, said : 'This is ridiculous' . . . and went out to clip two seconds off his time. To everyone's amazement Stewart went out again and calmly equalled the new pace. McLaren and Tyrrell knew they were watching a 'natural'.

Jackie Stewart was experiencing the same sort of inner glow that Graham Hill had felt when HE first drove a single seater car. 'I thought they were far too dangerous. I was only racing for fun anyway – in rather tired cars. That test drive changed my mind. Perhaps it was the exhilaration of driving such a precise machine. It seemed to do everything I wanted it to do. Perhaps it was just hunger for success, and, I must confess, a need constantly to test and prove myself.'

A few weeks later he was proving himself in top Formula Three company. His first race was on a miserable, wet day at Snetterton. By the end of the first lap Stewart led by over 300 yards. He couldn't believe it. He thought he must have jumped the flag.

It was to be the first of eleven runaway victories in thirteen races. Stewart had arrived. He says : 'I was very lucky to do my winning in 'warm-up' contests before the Grand Prix. All the Press were there and so were the team managers. I was a talking point because there were no other new faces around. I arrived at a lucky time.'

He was, of course, the target for the Grand Prix teams. Cooper, Lotus and BRM all wanted him. His canniness showed in his choice : he picked BRM 'Because I wanted to be in a team where they wouldn't rush me. They had a star in Graham Hill – I simply wanted to learn. Especially from him. I wanted my first year to be a year in which I could settle in at a sensible pace – not scramble for my career every time I arrived on the grid. I wanted to learn to handle a Formula One car. They aren't like other cars. They aren't forgiving if you make a mistake. You don't get a second chance. You are dealing with a thoroughbred.'

He was even more concerned about the DRIVERS he would have to face. As we flew out to his first Grand Prix, the South African Grand Prix in 1965, he confessed : 'Nine months ago these men were just names to me. Heroes that I looked up to. I still can't get used to the way they speak to me on level terms.' But he earned this equality. Sixth in his first race, he went on to win the International Trophy Race at Silverstone after a long battle with John Surtees in the Ferrari. He was second to Jim Clark in Belgium, France and Holland, and fifth in the British Grand Prix.

In the Italian Grand Prix at Monza he passed Graham Hill on the very last corner to take the victory flag for the first time. He was THIRD in the World Championship at his first attempt, with only the giants Jim Clark and Graham Hill – two men who befriended him like a kid brother – ahead of him.

BRM's £4,000 ($9,600) investment in the Formula Three star had proved money well spent. Stewart had not only lived up to every generous promise as a driver – but had emerged as a strong off-track personality too. He could sit at a table with Graham Hill and win his fair share of laughs. He was quick, buoyant and extremely quotable.

We sat one night at a tiny club near Chester where a well-endowed lady was gyrating madly to a twist band. In a transparent blouse, it was a fairly gruesome sight. Stewart cast an expert eye over the scene and declared : 'If she's not careful, she'll lap herself !'

He needed all his good humour in 1966. For though the year had begun well – with four Tasman victories and then a scorching win, the Monaco Grand Prix – there were bleaker days ahead. His first disappointment was at Indianapolis where he almost won the dollar-laden classic at his first attempt. He led from the 147th to the 192nd lap of the 200 lap race. A first time 'rookie' victory seemed imminent. Then a scavenger pump failed and Jackie had to stand glumly by as Graham Hill took the flag, the garlands – and the cheques.

In June we gathered at Spa, that awesome circuit in the

Ardennes where the weather can play such sudden and crucial tricks. The field roared off in the dry – and almost all disappeared. Back at the pits the wait seemed interminable before Surtees and Rindt appeared followed by one or two stragglers. What could have happened?

Four miles from the start the pack had howled into floods, caused by a local (very!) shower on the near, nine-mile circuit. Jo Bonnier, Mike Spence, Jo Siffert and Denny Hulme all spun off the track as their cars hit the rain. On the Masta Curve, Jackie Stewart disappeared in a cloud of spray, crashed into a ditch and lay trapped there with petrol flooding over him from split tanks.

This was the year that John Frankenheimer was filming 'Grand Prix', including Spa. But even this great director couldn't have staged the next sequence. Graham Hill roared into the same bend, spun wickedly and started gyrating backwards up the road like a top. When he came to a halt he peered into the ditch and there lay Stewart. Seconds later Hill was joined by the third BRM driver, Bob Bondurant, fresh from a ditch at the other side of the road – and between them they found help and tools. They undid the steering wheel that had trapped Stewart in the car, stripped off his clothing and generally made him safe and comfortable. But it was a horrifying experience. Just one spark . . . !

Jackie Stewart doesn't lack imagination and that accident has affected his racing ever since. He is without doubt the most safety-conscious driver on the circuits today. He was the first driver to wear a treated face mask – and it saved his features when oil sprayed across his mouth in New Zealand. He was the first driver to wear the new all-encasing helmet. He has been amongst the most earnest seekers after a fireproof driving suit which will give a driver more than seventeen seconds' grace in an explosion. He was the first Grand Prix driver to wear safety belts.

He has been unpopularly vociferous about the dangers of certain race circuits – notably Spa and Nürburgring. He just doesn't subscribe to the fatuous view aired by so-called aficionado that there have to be risks in racing. And if there are any risks, he will do everything in his power to minimise them.

After the Spa crash he insisted that a spanner was strapped to the BRM steering wheel. Today he has taken the unprecedented step of taking a leading surgeon – a resuscitation expert – to the circuits with him. It cost a lot of money but: 'I have only one life. Taking precautions won't make an accident happen. I'd just like to feel that if I ever had one – I'd have the best possible medical chance of surviving.'

Stewart rarely shows anger, but the taunts of people who claim that racing drivers have 'gone soft' because of their overwhelming preoccupation with safety do infuriate him. 'I'm not paid to risk my life – I'm paid to drive a racing car as fast as I can. And to live to drive it another day.'

Stewart suffered a broken shoulder, a cracked rib, skin burns and internal bruising from that crash at Spa. He returned to the fray for the British Grand Prix but the BRM H-16 simply wasn't reliable or competitive.

Graham Hill quit BRM at the end of the season and Jackie Stewart found himself the team leader of the all-British equipe. There followed another gloomy year. Ferrari approached him, but Ken Tyrrell was due to renew the partnership. The wily Tyrrell had helped the giant French Matra firm to gain a foothold in Formula Two racing and now felt ready to take the big gamble, to run a Grand Prix team.

Jackie had no hesitation in joining the experiment. The old firm were together again – and Matra had cause to be thankful that their Formula One project was in the hands of this redoubtable pair. This is not to say that it was roses all the way. In a Formula Two race in April 1968, Stewart crashed heavily into the wire mesh. The steering wheel twisted his wrist and snapped a bone. He had to miss the Spanish and Monaco Grand Prix and returned to Spa to drive one handed – using the bad wrist simply to change gear.

It was an incredible effort. Everyone thought he was out of his mind – particularly at Spa. But Stewart took the lead, built up a half-minute gap and then was halted with fuel starvation and further delayed by a flat battery. Yet he still finished fourth. The car was a good one. He could hardly wait for Holland, despite a swollen, painful wrist which definitely didn't approve of the bumps on the Zandvoort circuit.

Stewart had to miss a day's practice because of the pain and knew that he couldn't manage to finish the race if the track was dry. On race day his luck changed. It poured. And Stewart led for ninety laps, thankful that the wet track lightened the steering effort.

He was third in the French Grand Prix at Rouen and arrived at Brands Hatch knowing that Championship points were vital. It must have been this knowledge that kept him going on the cruelly bumpy British circuit. Says Jackie : 'I have never raced anywhere with such pain. I wanted to stop but I knew I needed points – no matter how few. I drove with one hand for at least half the race.'

It was a stoic effort that ended in utter exhaustion. Stewart had to be lifted from the car, was violently sick and slept for eighteen hours. But he had earned one point for finishing sixth – it could mean everything by the end of the season.

His doctors warned him to stop racing for a while and they must have known that Nürburgring – the scene for the German Grand Prix – would be the worst possible circuit for Stewart's arm. But Jackie was determined to race and once again rain gods made it easier for him . . . if you can describe a fog-bound battle through the Eifel mountains as 'easy'.

It was a grim and gruesome Grand Prix. The mist, fog and spray made every move a hazard. But Stewart grabbed a lead by the second lap and stormed away in a cloud of spray. He built up such a fantastic lead that it was FOUR MINUTES before the second car appeared through the gloom at the finish. 'It was undoubtedly my best performance' says Stewart, 'but it certainly wasn't the race of which I am most proud. I was not really in control of the situation. It was simply a big, teeth gritting effort.'

Of course it opened up the Championship. Stewart found himself only four points behind Graham Hill – bad arm and all. In Monza he retired, in Canada he was sixth, but he won the American Grand Prix with ease. Everything depended on Mexico. Stewart really had to win to prevent Graham Hill from taking the title – and the duel between the two friends and rivals made the first few laps knife-edge for the spectators. First Hill led, then Stewart, then Hill again. But Stewart's car went sick – for a trivial, infuriating reason. The pipe from one of the tanks became choked by a tiny piece of gauze. Stewart finished seventh, but Hill was already receiving the victory cheers. It was a cruelly disappointing end to the first Tyrrell/Matra/Stewart season. A season in which the diminutive Scot had showed grit of Graham Hill proportions as he battled on through pain and fatigue.

He had undoubtedly matured enormously. I talked to him in the Tyrrell pit while the champagne flowed in the Lotus camp. 'I just don't like getting so close,' he confessed. 'We mustn't let it happen again. Next season we'll settle it before Mexico.'

In retrospect, he admits that it was better for both motor racing and Jackie Stewart that Graham had taken the title. He didn't want to be dubbed 'boy wonder' – and there was no doubt that Hill's triumph in such a tragic season for Lotus caught the public imagination right round the world.

Stewart joined in the festivities; congratulated Hill with real warmth – and plotted a take over in 1969! He and Tyrrell started work on the next season's campaign almost immediately. They were in South Africa – testing relentlessly – before Hogmanay had ceased full flood in his native Scotland. No team was in a greater state of readiness; no team was so quietly confident by the time the 1969 season opened at Kyalami, in March. Stewart took the lead on the first corner and never looked like losing it.

In Spain he was downright lucky. Hill and Rindt crashed and the race was Chris Amon's until the Ferrari's engine failed. Stewart simply inherited the lead. His comments are a real guide to the inner honesty of the likeable Scot. 'It is the race of which I am least proud. In fact, I gave the trophy away the other day to the Guild of Motoring Writers. I felt as if I had stolen it. I gave it away, not because I didn't want it, but because it was a constant reminder of a race I won simply by being there. By sheer luck. I didn't have to be good to win that race. Ken Tyrrell could have won it driving our car! It was a fluke. So don't ever get big-headed. Sometimes you win and you aren't all that good.'

At Monte Carlo, Lady Luck compensated the unlucky Spanish combatants. Stewart lost a twenty second lead when the drive-shaft coupling broke and he could only stand and watch as Graham Hill won his FIFTH Monaco Grand Prix.

Stewart then went on to win the Dutch, the French and the British Grand Prix in barn-storming fashion. And his British victory was proof yet again of his resilience and self-discipline. On the final day's practice he smashed into a piece of concrete kerb on Silverstone's 140 mph Woodcote corner. His rear tyre exploded. The car smashed into the wall and although Stewart escaped unhurt, the car was a hopeless wreck. It was a very nasty accident indeed yet Stewart's first thought was to slow other cars down – and then to requalify for the race in team-mate Jean-Pierre Beltoise's car. Within an hour of the accident he had lapped fast enough in the borrowed car to earn a front-row, grid position.

At Nürburgring, Jackie finished second to Jacky Ickx – after driving much of the race with a damaged gearbox. Bruce McLaren was now Stewart's only real threat for the Championship. But at Monza Stewart was to put this issue beyond doubt – he wasn't going to wait for another nail-biting Mexico 'final' this year. In a tremendous slipstreaming battle with Jochen Rindt, with Hulme, Hill, Courage, McLaren, Siffert and Beltoise, all in the high-speed throng, Stewart won by .08 of a second. A few feet after 242.95 miles!

The title was his – five years after that epic test drive at Goodwood. And he had won it under the banner of the man who had first given him a chance to prove himself in a single seater – Ken Tyrrell. Stewart was dazed by his own success. 'I remember everyone else being more hilariously affected by the Monza victory than I was. I couldn't really appreciate the fact that I really was World Champion.

'It took a silly sort of incident to prove it to me. I had asked the concièrge at my hotel to book me a flight to Paris and I came downstairs next morning while he was doing it. He was having difficulties and then he said : "I want a seat on the plane for Jackie Stewart – the World Champion." Then I knew I really was Champion and thought "Isn't that nice?"

'You go numb for a while. I remember phoning my father after I had won it – and thinking he sounded thirty years younger. It wasn't just the title that affected me. It was knowing that I'd won it in a way that was important to me –

I'd won it convincingly. There's a great song by Frank Sinatra – "My Way". I think every man thinks of himself when he hears that particular song sung by Sinatra. But when I won the World Championship I remember listening to it afterwards and thinking, That's it – I have done it "my way". It's taken some ups and downs. You've been a pawn and you've been a king. I knew I'd be a pawn again someday – and then perhaps a king again. I had this terrific mental kaleidoscope of seeing my career in a very clear way and recognising that all had not been good and that certainly all had not been bad. I often look back and get a great feeling of pleasure that I tasted the thing I had been aiming for all those years.'

Jackie Stewart had fulfilled his personal ambition and made the critics happy. For once they had forecast a Champion accurately – although some of them had been a little premature! But no one had predicted the sort of Champion Stewart would become. Earlier in 1964 he had signed a contract with the giant Mark McCormack organisation: a deliberate step to mould himself into the complete commercial professional.

His off-circuit career became a hurricane of personal appearances, frank articles, documentaries, factory tours, sponsorships, quiz games and photo sessions. The purists blinked in disapproval. The more sympathetic said he would never stand the strain. Stewart rushed on – as though his personal batteries were being exhilaratingly re-charged by the new challenge and the bright new worlds he was determined to conquer.

'I have now learned to live a very busy life' he told me. 'And I get a great deal of pleasure out of it. If I was just a straight racing driver doing no appearances, no business with Ford Motor Company, Goodyear Tyres, Rolex Watches, and any of the people I am associated with, I might get bored. A few years of that would be quite enough. But it's not going to happen. Every six months something new and totally different arises for me to do. Another new challenge.'

In fact motor racing is no longer the main time-consumer in Stewart's life. 'The percentage of my life that I actually spend racing is, of course, very small. I spend so much time on business, appearances, photo sessions, doing films, commercials and travelling. I average 56 hours a month on a plane. That's 400,000 miles a year – more than an airline pilot flies. But they're not idle hours. I work while I am on a plane. I wrote columns for instance.'

Does motor racing still matter to Stewart then?

'Oh yes, I still love being a racing driver. I like driving racing cars. It is supposed to be old hat to say it gives you a lot of satisfaction and that there is nothing more exciting to do – but it nevertheless happens to be true. And motor racing is vital to me. It is the key to everything else that I do. If I am not competitive, a good racing driver, a winner – then I will no longer be wanted by these other people. It's a cruel world. People don't want you when you are not very good and I respect them for that. I don't expect to be used if I'm not supplying the goods. Motor racing is enormously important to me to the extent that I MUST be successful. I can't "con" my way into situations. Results still count. I must still perform well even though I don't always win. I must be leading. I must be setting the fastest lap. I must be considered to be the best, or amongst the best, racing drivers.'

There are some critics who would say that Stewart has reached the stage where he only 'uses' motor racing to further his other activities; that it is an unavoidable risk that publicises – yet at the same time – jeopardises the money-making, extra-mural bandwagons.

No one who has seen Stewart snuggle into a racing car, whether for tyre testing, practice, or the heat of real battle, would ever agree. Perhaps, in fact, the opposite is true. The excitement of commerce has prevented Stewart from going stale. It has kept the competitive edges honed.

At times the very bustle has preserved his sanity. For no one has suffered losses more keenly than Jackie Stewart. He says simply : '1970 was not a very nice year. We lost Jochen, Bruce and Piers. There were times when I didn't really enjoy my racing much. I was lifted out of this mood by my other activities. If I had just been left to soak in the sadness I might have gone off racing altogether as an emotional thing. I was never allowed to do that because I was too busy. The losses were never made small for me. But the medicine diluted the availability of time, of static time to weigh upon myself.'

The hardest race of Stewart's career was the Monza Grand Prix of 1970. There couldn't be a more bitter contrast to his feelings just twelve months earlier, when he went to the grid to become Champion : to beat Rindt and Piers Courage in a slip-streaming battle, to eliminate Bruce McLaren's last challenge for the crown.

Jochen Rindt, his friend, rival and neighbour, crashed and died the day before the race. Bruce McLaren and Piers Courage had been killed in the previous months.

'Jochen's death was the last straw. To have literally all my friends – with the exception of Graham – everyone that I had really known in racing, gone. Jimmy Clark's death had affected me terribly. But that was two years ago. Suddenly all the cuts seemed to be coming up on one day and they were just gashed open. I just wasn't able to take it. I have never felt less like driving. I have never felt so totally drained – drained utterly of emotion, of feeling, of life – as when I drove that race. I went through a big emotional thing that I had not experienced before. I won my race ... I did not win the race itself. I was second. Maybe I should have won the race. But it was a little out of my control. But I won my race. There were four of us fighting for second place and I beat them. And when I had finished I was a destroyed man, a totally destroyed man. I had had to inject a build-up into my own system – into my own mind. It was a very important point in my career. I think only a handful of people realised it was the most important race I had ever run.'

The popular, public image of the bouncing, quip-a-minute Scot exposes no inkling of this fine, occasionally raw, sensitivity. There is nothing special about a man who suffers when his firmest friends are killed. But there is something extraordinary about a man who can voluntarily submit himself to the same risks within hours of a stunning, grievous loss. There can be no trite parallel with the wartime pilot or infantry hero.

There is no outside force to compel a racing driver to return to the cockpit. Just a personal philosophy that bewilders the outsider. Says Stewart : 'I carry on because motor racing is a disease. You can be distraught with sadness and sorrow because of people you have lost when suddenly you have a mental injection and you get into your racing car. At that time you are totally anaesthetised. The past doesn't exist and while you are in a racing car nothing happens. There are no memories, no past – you don't think of these things at all.

'It's very infectious. It carries you beyond thinking of these things. Now I think of Jochen, Jimmy, Piers and Bruce in a way that I have adjusted my mind to – a new way. I think all racing drivers do this. I think I am still a very sensitive person. It's simply been a case of finding ways to handle it – finding keys that fit. That do the trick, but don't make me feel hard and cold about it. I still spend an awful lot of time with Jochen's wife Nina and their daughter. And I can do it without detesting racing. I think racing allows you to do this, and I think it's unique in this respect.'

There is another, more positive side to the Stewart philosophy. Motor racing not only blunts the senses when sorrow grinds in, but gives them a finer edge with which to appreciate the happier experience.

'My whole appreciation of life has been intensified by motor racing. I enjoy my life in such an intense way that it frightens me sometimes. I think to myself : "Jesus, I just can't continue to enjoy myself to this extent for long. There's something wrong. It can't be this good" and when things are so good you wonder when they are all going to stop.'

Above all, Stewart enjoys driving a racing car. Testing himself and the machine at the limit. 'I still adore the feeling that I am in control of the situation. I still get great anticipation if it has just started to rain in practice for instance. I really do want to go out and do a few laps.

'Although I hate it, there is a funny little machine that goes off inside that says even if you hate it – and are slightly frightened by it – you still want to go out and do it. It's a special ingredient that motor racing supplies that no other sport has. It has this double header on it : one side is danger, one is wanting to do it.'

Few drivers are as frank about their motives as Stewart. But his total awareness about his own strange compulsions have helped him to see the dangers and to guard against them as much as is physically possible. He has no illusions. One day he will stop motor racing – and it could be a very sudden decision.

'If I ever woke up in the morning and found that motor racing was giving me a bad taste in my mouth – like a bad oyster – I'd stop at once. Even if it was the morning of a big race. I think motor racing is such a thing that if you feel that way you must stop at once. I think you would be doing your duty to your family, to yourself and the people who are paying you. If you go in and your heart is totally against it, then that's the time you get nervous. That's the time you do stupid things. And that's the time you get killed. If I ever felt that way I would stop at once. And money would have no consideration at all.'

To date, however, there is little sign that the Stewart appetite for racing, and the dizzy array of extra-mural activities dependent on it, is soured in any way. In 1971 he was sharper than ever. He simply monopolised the World Championship with six crushing victories that gave him a runaway, second title.

He seems totally in command. A master of the media as well as the machinery of racing. At the Silverstone International Trophy Meeting in May 1971 he crashed at over 100 mph at Copse corner. He was out of the car in seconds ran back to turn off the ignition and minutes later was giving a concise, controlled TV account of the whole incident. As if that wasn't enough, he glanced over the pit rail, watched the leaders pass – and accurately forecast: 'Graham Hill will win the race'. And this at a time when Hill was trailing Rodriguez.

He is, without a doubt, a natural. A born driver who has applied himself to every peripheral art of racing so that he is a master of any situation on or off the track. Whenever he decides to quit racing he will certainly never return to the petrol pumps of the family garage.

Stewart could make a living as a salesman, businessman, columnist, disc-jockey, fashion writer or commentator. He has personality, wit, courage, independence, application, an open mind and highly astute judgment. And his opinions, like his conversation in general, are never dull. At the end of this book it is interesting to hear the fastest contemporary driver's assessments of the men he has watched, and admired, from afar. And the men against whom he has raced. Who are the 'Grand Prix Greats' in Stewart's personal file? Without hesitation he told me:

'FANGIO because I think he is the man I must respect. He is a diplomat. He had enormous talent. He had great feeling –

he still has. He is a quiet man, he is not a bombastic man. He is an artist and he is quite happy to know he is an artist without having to tell everybody. They already know it anyway. He's modest. He shows great balance and great judgment in his life. He's a nice man. He's a super man and he's still an electric man. JIMMY CLARK because he had a talent above everybody else I knew at the time I was racing against him. He had this beautiful driving ability together with other failings in life that he had to conquer. The strength he had to conquer them showed enormous character and self-respect. And he didn't care sometimes if other people objected to what he was doing. He knew what he had to do. He was the complete Grand Prix driver. He had enormous natural ability. He was a complete gentleman; the drivers' driver.

'STIRLING MOSS because he did so much as a driving talent. He was the greatest driver and I don't think he ever believed he was the greatest driver while he was doing it. He was confident but he was always wanting better things to be sure he would win. He was the great natural. He's still doing a great job for racing today. He still seems the same. Stirling Moss was a racing driver. People wanted racing drivers to look like Stirling Moss. He was THE one. Irrespective of what else he was, he was a good driver – and he was good at the other things he did, too.

'JOCHEN RINDT. In my opinion Jochen had incredible talent. It took some time for it to develop into a winning talent but it was always there. The greatest thing about Jochen for me was his great strength of character, because he didn't care a damn what anybody thought. If he thought somebody was an idiot he told them they were an idiot and that was it: the case was closed! He wasn't influenced by other people; he wasn't influenced if they had money – it was just the fact that they were idiots. Nobody could tell you that somebody was an idiot more clearly than Jochen. And it was his own judgment and his own values that this was based on. Nothing to do with anybody else or reading books or anything else. It was Jochen's opinion. He was a natural. He was very purposeful. And he was also a very gentle man which few people saw. He had great respect and great feeling for a few people and these few people he would do anything for – beyond the kind of things that people would credit Jochen for. Well beyond it. People haven't given Jochen the credit he deserves. I think he is getting it now.'

Jackie paused : 'These four to me are outstanding.'

There was one more obvious question. Where would he place John Young Stewart? 'I don't know,' he said honestly, 'I'd be very proud to be amongst those four.'

There is no doubt in my mind that, both on and off the tack, he has more than qualified. The statistics show that only Jim Clark and Fangio have scored more than his 18 Grand Prix victories. And 1972 could see Stewart outpace both these 'greats' in the record books.

For like both of them – he is quite simply the most outstanding driver of his age.

The only question mark against a dizzy total of achievements is his own desire to continue. At the end of a season where 40,000 gathered to pay tribute to the Scot's triumphs at Brands Hatch – and left mourning Jo Siffert – Stewart talked more frankly than ever before.

'I can see the horizon now,' he told me. 'I know what lies ahead of me. I can see a day when I will stop.

'But I won't leave motor racing altogether. I'd like to stay in the sport. I'd like to be involved with some scheme to help develop young drivers. I want to stay around.'

His mind was buzzing. The ideas were flowing. He was already looking for new horizons to conquer.

And Jackie Stewart is still only thirty-two-years-old. The one-time clay pigeon Champion and all-time great driver could well have another, third, career conquered by the time he is forty.

Motor racing enthusiasts can only hope that he will pack in a few more classic victories before he decides to step out of the cockpit for good. And that like Fangio and Brabham – but unlike so many of the other immortals in this book – he will escape to 'retirement' unscathed.

Then it will be a case of sitting back and waiting for something new to happen. One thing alone is certain : whatever he chooses to do, he will do it thoroughly, professionally and a damned sight better than most other folk.

And it will be fascinating to watch him do it !

# INDEX